Evaluating State EITC Options for California

• • •

Thomas MaCurdy

2004

Public Policy Institute *of* California
1994–2004

Library of Congress Cataloging-in-Publication Data
  MaCurdy, Thomas E.
    Evaluating state EITC options for California / Thomas MaCurdy.
    p. cm.
    ISBN 1-58213-068-X
    1. Earned income tax credit—California. I. Title.

HJ4655.C23C735 2004
336.24'216—dc22   2004004500

Foreword

When he was governor of California, Ronald Reagan supported the idea of an earned income tax credit (EITC). President Ford signed a bill instituting it in 1975, and President Clinton greatly expanded the concept in 1993. As a consequence of this bipartisan support over the last 30 years, the EITC has become one of the largest anti-poverty programs in the United States. Initially, the EITC was established to offset the adverse effects of Social Security and Medicare payroll taxes on working poor families. Today, more money (about $30 billion in FY2000) is spent on EITC than on Temporary Assistance for Needy Families (TANF), and over 20 million people claim the credit annually. Unlike TANF, however, it rewards only those who are working. For the program's proponents, the greatest attraction of the EITC is that it strengthens the incentive to work by increasing the remuneration from low-paid jobs.

This remarkable program has also gained the attention of state governments, 17 of which now augment the federal tax credit levels. This augmentation is especially attractive because states can piggyback on the filing of federal income tax forms. To date, California has not adopted a "local" option. In *Evaluating State EITC Options for California*, Thomas MaCurdy analyzes different approaches to augmenting the national program and concludes that if California wishes to implement its own EITC, it should not simply "add on" to the federal plan. Rather, it should design a program that considers a family's hourly wages as well as its earnings. He systematically reviews four options along the same criteria and observes that a state EITC plan that considers both wages and earnings can better target low-wage families and encourage additional hours of work. Although administratively more complex than a simple add-on to earnings, such a plan would better serve low-wage California families and the state's income-support programs and goals.

It is worth noting how far income-support policies have evolved since the mid-1970s. At that time, the negative income tax generated a heated debate in the Nixon White House and in both houses of Congress. It was eventually rejected for its potential to dampen work incentives and disrupt families. Passed in the midst of that debate, the EITC today provides a substantial amount of income support with only a modest effect on work incentives. In effect, a good part of the negative income tax is with us today as the EITC. For those not in the workforce, welfare reform passed in the 1990s addressed some of the worst aspects of the old welfare programs—the very ones that were the target of the negative income tax movement. Term limits combined with generous work training and child care benefits resulted from the passage of TANF, and so we now see an income-support package for working and nonworking poor families that addresses the tradeoffs that bedeviled the negative income tax. Public policy changes are usually evolutionary rather than revolutionary, and the emergence of EITC as a significant anti-poverty program for America is a good example of this pattern.

As California comes to grips with its formidable budget deficits, it will no doubt return its attention to the normal business of government, which includes ensuring effective and efficient markets for labor, land, and finance. Augmenting the national EITC program may well be one of the best approaches to ensuring a productive supply of labor for generations to come. MaCurdy's report provides the blueprint for designing just such a program.

David W. Lyon
President and CEO
Public Policy Institute of California

Summary

In recent years, a number of states have developed their own state earned income tax credit (EITC) to supplement the federal EITC. The federal EITC is a refundable credit, administered through the income tax system, and designed to ensure that full-time low-wage work would bring a family above the poverty line. The federal EITC has a phasein range, where the size of the credit rises with earnings; a plateau, where the credit does not change with earnings; and a phaseout range, where the credit falls with earnings. As recently as 2001, the California legislature has considered a California EITC. Like other states, it has proposed an EITC structured to provide an additional credit equal to a share of the federal EITC payment. Figure S.1 shows the structure of the federal EITC with a state supplement of 15 percent.

A state EITC offers an opportunity to further reward work for low-income families with children. However, designing an optimal EITC is

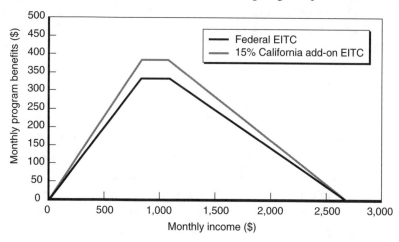

Figure S.1—Monthly Benefits from a 15 Percent California Add-On to the Federal Earnings-Based EITC Program for a Family with Two Children

far more challenging than most would surmise, especially if policymakers take into account interactions with other federal and state programs. As with any income-support program, there are inherent tradeoffs among the cost of a program, the benefits to recipients, and the returns to work. A well-targeted program with minimal work disincentives can provide appreciable benefits to those who receive the EITC and minimize the costs. This report considers the design features of alternative EITC structures to assess which EITC may come closest to such an optimal design, accounting for the particular incentives currently built into the social safety net in California.

The "add-on" state EITC design has been the most popular choice among states implementing state EITCs, where most offer a benefit equal to 10 percent to 25 percent of the federal credit. Recent California bills, such as AB 106 (Cedillo) in the 2000–2001 session, have proposed a 15 percent state supplement to federal EITC benefits. The popularity of this design is largely due to the administrative ease; because expenditures on the federal EITC are known, it is also easy to predict the cost of this option. However, two states have selected different strategies, distributing benefits across poor and near-poor families in a way that differs from the federal allocation.

This report assesses the effectiveness of state EITC options along three dimensions: their effect on work incentives, the distribution of benefits across poor families and other family types, and the costs of such programs. As example cases, this study examines variations on four candidate EITC structures:

1. A simple "add-on" to the federal EITC program as recently proposed, supplementing federal benefits by a fixed percentage;
2. An earnings-based EITC that pays benefits in specific earnings ranges that differ systematically from the federal schedule, for example, targeting only low- or higher-earnings ranges;
3. A modified EITC that makes benefits dependent on wage levels *and* earnings to lessen work disincentives; and
4. An EITC that emulates a minimum wage through a tax credit that phases out with earnings to prevent benefits from going to high-income families.

These effects are analyzed using two distinct strategies. To understand the effects on work incentives, we first model the work incentives in existing programs and then evaluate how EITC options would improve or worsen existing incentives. The distribution of benefits and the total costs of programs are predicted through simulations on comprehensive data on California families in 1999 from the Survey of Income and Program Participation collected by the U.S. Census Bureau.

The first two design options can be described as earnings-based EITCs. Under these options, the benefits to families with children are determined solely by earnings and income, paying the same benefits to low-wage families working full-time as to families working half as much at double the wage. Earnings-based EITCs can be simple supplements to the federal EITC or can use different income ranges to target benefits, supplementing only low earnings, or going into effect only for earnings nearest the poverty threshold. These designs are shown as the first three options on Figure S.2, which describes the share of benefits going to selected groups of families. Key findings on these earnings-based EITC options are listed below.

- A 15 percent add-on EITC does little to improve work incentives, especially serious disincentives for full-time work experienced by CalWORKs and Food Stamps recipients. Qualified families would receive $305 per year on average, and the program could cost more than $730 million annually if all eligible families participate.
- A "high-earnings" EITC, targeted close to the poverty threshold, would encourage employed CalWORKs families to work the additional hours required to leave aid. If the maximum were set at the same 15 percent, this option would cost 40 percent less than the add-on EITC. Because fewer families would receive the maximum benefit, the average benefit would be $256 annually.
- A "low-earnings" EITC, targeted at the lowest levels of earnings, would best target poor families, again at substantial savings over the add-on option, about half the cost. Average benefits would be similar to those in the high-earnings option.

Options 3 and 4 listed above allow formulations that can significantly improve both work incentives and the targeting of resources to working poor families. The fundamental idea in these "wage-linked" proposals is to make EITC benefits depend on a family's hourly wages (averaged over all workers) as well as its earnings. This change allows designs far better targeted to low-wage workers and to full-time work, because families with low earnings from high wages but low work effort are less likely to benefit. The "wage-based EITC" provides a share of the maximum EITC benefit based on the share of full-time work, so a family working full-time receives the full 15 percent supplement, but a family working half-time receives only half as much. Wage-subsidy EITCs pay the difference between the market wage earned by a worker and a threshold wage, such as $7.50 per hour, for up to 40 hours per week of work. This subsidy can be phased out beyond the equivalent of full-time work or workers may be allowed to keep the maximum subsidy even if they (or family members combined) work more than full-time. Key findings on these wage-linked EITCs, shown as the last three options on Figure S.2, are listed below.

- The wage-based EITC offers virtually identical income support and work incentives for the lowest-wage workers, and it enhances returns to work for moderate- and higher-wage workers working less than full-time. This option costs just over three-quarters the expense of the add-on EITC, because it lowers the benefits paid to families working part-time and families working for higher wages.
- The wage-subsidy EITC makes payments only to families supported by low-wage jobs. A wage-subsidy that includes a phaseout of benefits above full-time work costs somewhat more than the add-on EITC but provides more than four times the benefits to qualifying families. A wage-subsidy EITC improves incentives for additional work, including helping families working their way off welfare.
- The wage-subsidy EITC operates as if a state minimum wage law were passed applying only to low-income families with children, so it is far better than a minimum wage in targeting

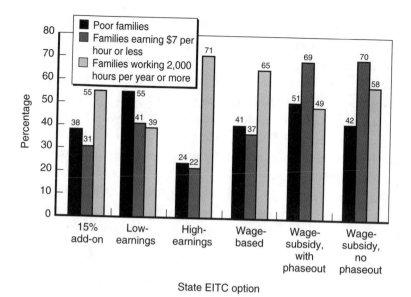

Figure S.2—Share of State EITC Benefits Provided to Families
with Children, by Family Characteristics

workers supporting children on low wages, at a substantially
lower cost. Of course, the costs of the EITC are directly
observed in the tax-transfer system, rather than paid by
consumers and business owners. Families combining part-time
work and welfare benefit more from the EITC, because welfare
benefits are not reduced by the EITC.

Thus, EITC structures that account for both wages and earnings can
better target benefits to low-wage families and encourage additional
hours of work. These strategies, of course, lack the administrative
simplicity of the add-on EITC. The biggest administrative challenges to
a wage-linked EITC are identifying hourly wages or hours of work,
especially for families with multiple workers. These would not seem to
be insurmountable barriers, however, because average wages used to be
reported as part of California's unemployment program, and the
structure of the program is not very sensitive to different rules for
assigning wages within families.

The lessons of this report indicate that policymakers should de-link a California EITC from the federal program to accomplish the goals they deem of priority in establishing the policy. The exact structure will have to be determined by weighing the tradeoffs among the competing goals of targeting support, enhancing work incentives, and keeping overall program costs low. Although most other states have opted for a simple add-on to the federal EITC, the needs of California families and the structures of California's income-support programs will be better served by a more innovative approach for California's earned income tax credit. In this regard, designing a state EITC that accounts for a family's hourly wages as well as its earnings in the determination of benefits offers vital features enabling more precise attainment of designated goals.

Contents

Figures

Tables

Acknowledgments

The author gratefully acknowledges research support from the Public Policy Institute of California for this project, as well as supplemental support provided by the Smith-Richardson Foundation, by the Donner Foundation, and by a grant from the National Institutes of Health. Many thanks to Dana Rapoport and Peggy O'Brien-Strain for their substantial assistance revising and editing the report. Thanks also for the helpful comments from Hilary Hoynes, Maureen Waller, Fred Silva, and, most especially, Eileen Rousch. Opinions expressed in this report are those of the authors and do not represent the official position or policy of any agency funding this research.

1. Introduction

In recent years, California Assembly and Senate policy committees have considered a number of bills to introduce a state earned income tax credit (EITC) to supplement the federal EITC.[1] At both the state and federal levels, the chief appeal of the EITC is that it subsidizes low-income families who support themselves through earnings rather than public assistance. The federal EITC, originally designed to offset payroll taxes, was significantly enhanced in the mid-1990s, when the EITC was increased to ensure that full-time low-wage work would bring a family above the poverty line. As a refundable credit, the EITC provides assistance to families even if they do not face any tax liability. The federal program is administered by the Internal Revenue Service, and families receive the credit as a refund on their federal income taxes. A number of states have developed their own earned income tax credits, several in response to welfare reform, recognizing that the EITC encourages welfare recipients to achieve self-sufficiency.

Throughout the 1990s, "making work pay" became a centerpiece of both state and federal policies implemented to assist poor families. Most programs developed during this time incorporated features aimed at encouraging families to work. The 1993 expansion of the federal EITC represents the most prominent example, for it explicitly ties benefits to work. Today, the EITC constitutes the largest federal cash or near-cash assistance program for low-income households, far outdistancing expenditures on "welfare" programs such as Temporary Assistance for Needy Families (TANF) and Food Stamps. In California, CalWORKs (California Work Opportunity and Responsibility to Kids— the state's version of TANF introduced in 1997 as part of welfare reform) also

---

[1]The key example is AB 106 (Cedillo) in the 2001–2002 session. Senator Solis and Assembly Members Solis, Ducheny, Wiggins, and Villaraigosa have also offered state EITC proposals. Information on bills can be found on the state's legislative website at www.leginfo.ca.gov.

encourages beneficiaries to acquire employment through work requirements and time limits. Moreover, both CalWORKs and the Food Stamps program incorporate "earnings disregards" in their benefit structure as a way to reward part-time work. Not to be overlooked, policymakers have increased both the federal and state minimum wages several times since the mid-1990s, citing alleviation of poverty and encouraging work as the primary motivations for such policy.

Structuring policies that both promote work effort and target benefits to poor families is far more challenging than most would surmise. Such policies inherently involve weighing tradeoffs among three goals: (1) targeting support to particular categories of families, (2) providing work incentives encouraging families to attain self-sufficiency, and (3) keeping overall program costs low. Understanding these tradeoffs is complicated by the interaction of each new policy with other federal and state income-support systems. Policymakers must be aware of these tradeoffs to achieve the desired balance in programs to assist working poor families.

Existing programs offer a decidedly mixed record in attaining this balance. The federal EITC targets benefits to low-earnings families, but these families need not be low-wage earners. Moreover, the EITC sharply discourages full-time work for relatively moderate-wage families and those with more than one worker. Work disincentives grow substantially for all EITC families who also collect Food Stamps, and they can render incremental work effort virtually uncompensated if a family also receives CalWORKs benefits. Raising the minimum wage does not avoid these tradeoffs. Although this policy typically enhances work incentives, the vast majority of its benefits go to nonpoor families and its implicit costs are considerable.

This study documents the features and embedded tradeoffs of current income-support programs, and it proposes several alternatives available to California for designing a state EITC that mitigates or avoids the adverse characteristics of existing policies. In particular, the analysis assesses the effects of four distinct candidate formulations for a state EITC:

1. A simple "add on" to the federal EITC program that supplements federal benefits by a fixed percentage;
2. An earnings-based EITC that pays benefits in specific earnings ranges that differ systematically from the federal schedule;
3. A modified EITC that makes benefits dependent on wage levels *and* earnings to lessen work disincentives; and
4. An EITC that emulates a minimum wage through a tax credit that phases out with earnings to prevent benefits going to high-income families.

California proposals have called for an add-on EITC, the first option, which is the same design as used in virtually all state EITCs. Only Indiana and Minnesota have different designs, both of which would fall under category 2.

The subsequent discussion addresses three questions that determine the effectiveness of different options for a state EITC in California:

- To what degree do existing policies encourage or discourage work?
- How are the benefits of programs distributed across different types of families, as characterized by wage levels, marital status, presence of children, welfare recipiency, and hours worked?
- Can variants of a state EITC program improve either work incentives or the targeting of benefits to particular populations?

The analysis of work incentives builds on an examination of the incentives in existing income-support programs. To evaluate the distributional effects of alternative EITC designs, this study simulates families' receipt of benefits using a sample of California families from the 1999 wave of the 1996 Survey of Income and Program Participation (SIPP) collected by the U.S. Census Bureau.

Five chapters make up the remainder of this study. Chapter 2 reviews both the federal and state income-support programs currently available in California and the effects of these programs on work incentives. Chapter 3 details specific versions of the four EITC structures to be considered in the analysis. Chapter 4 analyzes how the alternative state EITC designs would change rewards for additional work. Chapter 5 examines the distribution of the benefits provided by these programs across different possible target populations. Finally, Chapter 6 summarizes our findings and offers some concluding comments.

2. Work Incentives in Current Policies Supporting Working Poor Families

Because it is targeted to working poor families with children, a state EITC must be considered in concert with the existing programs serving such families. As a foundation to understand the effect of alternative state EITC policies, this chapter first reviews the benefit schedules of the primary income-supplement programs funded by the federal and state governments to assist working poor families in California. Taking these benefit schedules, we then evaluate the work incentives—or disincentives—embodied in the existing programs.

Current Income-Support Programs

Among the numerous federal programs offering income support to particular categories of families, the EITC, Food Stamps, and TANF programs play the most prominent role in attempts to alleviate poverty for working poor families with children. Through the block grants, TANF policy is largely determined by state policies, so CalWORKs is the major state program providing cash support for low-income families. Although it is not typically classified as an income-transfer program, the minimum wage is another vehicle often cited by both federal and state policymakers as an option for alleviating poverty for the working poor. Each of these policies provides different returns to work for low-income families.

Federal EITC Benefits

The federal EITC is principally set up to benefit working poor families who have children.[1] As shown in Figure 2.1, the benefit structure of the EITC targets the working poor by increasing as earnings rise to a prescribed level, then plateauing over a range of incomes, and, finally, declining steadily to zero. In this and subsequent figures, monthly earnings are graphed along the horizontal axis and monthly program benefits are along the vertical axis, so for each level of monthly earnings, we can assess the value (per month) of the tax credit. As the two lines depict, there is one benefit structure for families with one child and another for those with two or more children.

We can think of the benefits from the EITC from two distinct perspectives. First, we can think of a family being at some *fixed* income. Given this income on the horizontal axis, we can use the figure to determine the program benefits at that fixed income. From this perspective, setting up a benefit structure entails determining how much money we want the program to provide families of different incomes to

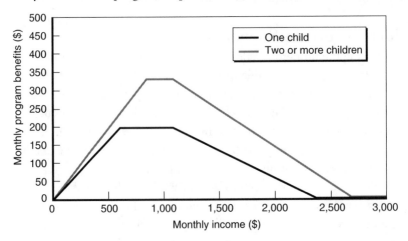

Figure 2.1—Monthly Benefits from the Federal Earnings-Based EITC Program for Different Family Sizes

---

[1]Although families without children can qualify for a small credit, this study concentrates on the much larger credits given to families with children.

help "make ends meet." Holding families' incomes constant, this perspective tells us how benefits would be distributed across families.

Consider an alternative perspective, however: Imagine a single mother deciding how many hours to work. Her net income depends on how many hours of work she chooses to complete at the best wage she can receive. From her perspective, this figure helps to decide at *which* income she obtains the best deal. Should she work a little and receive the maximum benefits from the program, or should she receive fewer benefits by working more hours, thus sacrificing free time with her children in return for a higher net income? For a mother not in the labor force, her choice may be whether to work part-time or full-time. For a mother working part-time, her choice may be whether to work additional hours. It is the same decision that each worker makes but with the added complication that she gains or loses money from the EITC according to the amount of money she earns from additional hours of work.

Under the federal EITC, a two-child family moving from no earnings to $840 a month finds that benefits rise sharply as earnings rise. Over this range, families have strong incentives to earn more as the government effectively provides "matching funds" of 40 cents for each dollar earned. Earning a dollar increases net income by $1.40 before taxes. Benefits plateau between $840 and $1,100 in monthly income. Families earning in that range get a little over $300 dollars a month from the EITC. Families earning more than $1,100 per month start losing money. Here, the phaseout rate—the rate at which benefits are lost—is about 21 cents on the dollar. So for every dollar a family earns over $1,100, it loses 21 cents in benefits. In other words, a dollar earned increases net income by only 79 cents (before payroll taxes). This pattern continues until all benefits are gone, at approximately $2,700 per month. At that point, the program no longer affects the family.

Food Stamps Benefits

Working poor families are also usually eligible for assistance through the Food Stamps program, which gives poor families coupons that can be redeemed for food. The exact amount of the benefit varies by the size of the family, monthly earnings, and various other exemptions. Figure 2.2

shows the value of the Food Stamps received by a single parent with either one or two children.

Because it is designed primarily to alleviate poverty rather than to reward work, the Food Stamps program provides different incentives for families than does the EITC. For a family with two children, Food Stamps benefits start out slightly less than $350 a month (a little higher than the maximum EITC benefit) for a family with no monthly income and stay at this level until the family makes more than $500 a month. From there, benefits drop at a constant rate with the family losing about 24 cents in Food Stamps for each dollar earned. This decline continues until benefits cut off at a monthly income of nearly $1,500.[2]

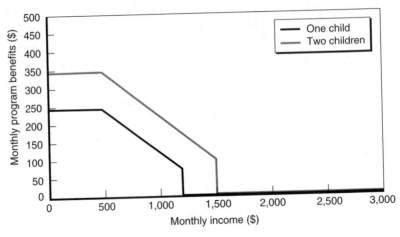

Figure 2.2—Monthly Benefits from Food Stamps for Different Family Sizes

---

[2]To illustrate the interaction of Food Stamps incentives and the EITC, our calculations are a generalized example of the Food Stamps rules. The calculations for Food Stamps use 2001 benefit levels presuming a single parent with children not on welfare and not claiming any child care credits. We use the fair market rent values set at the maximum allowable level for the Food Stamps program. Although these rent values are higher than average, this effect is mitigated by the fact that we do not account for child care deductions. Choosing a lower rent value would cause the benefits to phase out at a steeper slope over a shorter range; it also can cause benefits to begin phasing out earlier. The maximum benefits do not change, nor does the income level above which benefits fall to zero.

CalWORKs

The principal cash-transfer program funded by California to support its low-income families is CalWORKs. CalWORKs is a means-tested program designed to help families with children through direct cash aid. As with Food Stamps, benefits depend on family size and earnings. CalWORKs operates like the Food Stamps program, although its benefit levels and phaseout rate are much higher.

Figure 2.3 shows the CalWORKs benefits received by a single parent with either one or two children. Looking at the two-child family, benefits are fixed at about $650 per month for those with monthly earnings below $225, because the first $225 in earnings are "disregarded" in calculating benefits as an inducement for families to work. For those making more than $225, benefits decline 50 cents for every dollar earned. This reduction continues until benefits hit zero for families earning at least $1,500 per month. One-child families face the same phaseout rate and earnings disregard, but their initial benefits start out at slightly less than $525 per month.

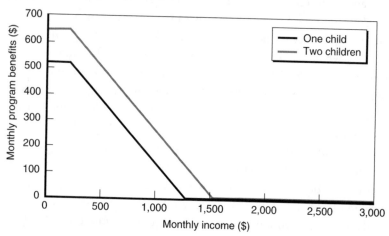

Figure 2.3—Monthly Benefits from the CalWORKs Program for Different Family Sizes

9

Federal and State Minimum Wages

The minimum wage is often touted as a strategy for increasing the earnings of poor families without spending federal or state money. For families relying on the work of a minimum-wage worker, increases in the minimum wage raise the income of the family. The current California minimum wage is $6.75 an hour, up from $6.25 in 2001. This is $1.60 above the current federal minimum wage of $5.15 per hour. The EITC effectively targets poor families, but it does not necessarily target low-wage workers because it depends only on total earnings and not hours of work. The principal advantage of the minimum wage is that it targets low-wage workers quite well. Its disadvantages are that it does not target poor families very well, and it may increase unemployment or impose other costs on many of the families it is intended to help.[3]

Work Incentives in Existing Low-Income Support Programs

Families receiving income support through the EITC, Food Stamps, or CalWORKs have higher income with the programs than they would have in the absence of such programs. However, these programs, especially when taken together, may have significant effects on the incentives to work. A program provides an incentive for an additional hour of work when the benefits add onto the hourly wage. A program provides a disincentive for an additional hour of work when the benefits fall with the additional wages. The exact incentives for additional work depend greatly on the starting level of earnings. In this section, we consider the extent to which current federal and state income-maintenance programs discourage work. Our base "no assistance" case examines the effects of income and payroll taxes on workers' earnings. We then consider work incentives for families who collect only EITC

---

[3]O'Brien-Strain and MaCurdy (2000) show that (1) families in poverty receive only a fraction of the benefits of a minimum-wage increase (less than 10 percent of additional earnings go to families with children supported primarily by minimum-wage earnings), and (2) low-income families face a larger percentage increase than high-income families in the price of goods they buy because an increase in the minimum wage drives up prices.

benefits, those who participate in both the EITC and the Food Stamps program, and, finally, those who participate in EITC, the Food Stamps program, and CalWORKs. As representative cases, our analysis assumes single-parent households with two children.

Rewards from Additional Hours Worked with Only Income/Payroll Taxes

The federal and state income and payroll taxes that all families pay on their earnings lower the incentives to work. Marginal rates depend not only on the level of earnings but also on the taxpayer's marital and head of household status and the number of dependents allotted to him or her. The 2001 federal tax code has five ranges of marginal tax rates: 10, 15, 27.5, 30.5, and 35.5 percent brackets. The 2001 rules also allow for a tax credit of $600 per child.[4] California income taxes include 1, 2, 4, 6, 8, and 9.3 percent brackets. The calculations below assume standard deductions for both the federal and state income taxes. For a single parent with two children, federal taxes (excluding the EITC) are zero until earnings exceed $2,200 a month, and state taxes are zero until earnings exceed $3,000 a month. Thus, a minimum-wage earner with two children does not pay income taxes until he or she works beyond full-time. Even a parent earning $12 per hour would have to work more than full-time to owe any federal or state taxes. The payroll tax, in contrast, takes 7.65 percent of earnings starting at the first dollar and thus affects all workers.

Because our focus is on the incentives for additional hours of work, we summarize the effects of the tax and transfer programs by plotting "effective" or "net" hourly wages: how much a worker earns in disposable income for each hour worked per week (assuming 50 weeks of work per year). Figure 2.4 plots the effective hourly wage of two workers whose families pay income and payroll taxes but do not participate in EITC or any other welfare programs. To isolate the effects of low wages and low earnings, we consider workers at two different wage levels: One earns a

---

[4]The 2003 tax cuts make additional reductions in marginal tax rates and increases in the child tax credits. California has considered additional high-income tax brackets for its 2003–2004 budget. For consistency, we will follow rules effective in 2001.

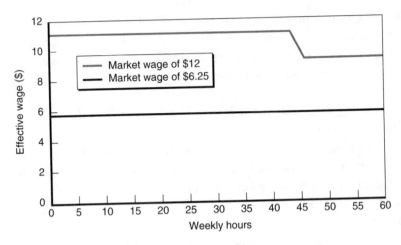

Figure 2.4—Effective Wage after Taxes

gross wage of $6.25 per hour (the minimum wage prevailing in 2001), and the second earns $12 per hour.

As we see on Figure 2.4, payroll taxes are deducted from the minimum-wage earner's paycheck but these workers do not earn enough to pay income taxes unless they work more than 80 hours per week. Their effective wage, accounting for payroll and income taxes, is $5.77 per hour, no matter how many hours are worked in the 0 to 60 hour range, showing up as a straight line on the figure. With the 2001 expansion of the child tax credit and adoption of lower marginal tax rates, a single parent with two children first pays income taxes when annual earnings reach $26,400, equivalent to $2,200 per month. The second worker depicted in Figure 2.4, who earns $12 per hour, hits the income tax threshold working just under 42 hours per week. For hours worked above 42 per week, take-home pay for an additional hour of work falls from $11.08 with only payroll taxes to $9.28 with payroll taxes plus income taxes.

Effects of the EITC on the Effective Wages of Working Families

Because of the phasein, plateau, and phaseout portions of the EITC, rewards to work vary according to how much families earn. When a family has low hours and earnings, the EITC subsidizes wages by providing a tax credit for each dollar earned. After a particular point, however, the EITC reduces benefits paid to a family for each additional dollar it earns; as a result, it acts like a conventional income or payroll tax. In this range of hours and earnings, the family's disposable income rises by less than its earnings.

The different ranges of the federal EITC complicate the graph of effective wages. Figure 2.5 adds the federal EITC to payroll and income taxes, plotting the effective or net hourly wages for the same two workers. For both of these workers, the effective wage for an additional hour of work in the lowest range of hours is higher than their market wage, creating an incentive for additional work in this range. For workers working less than approximately 32 hours per week, those earning a market wage of $6.25 take home an effective wage of $8.27 per hour, reflecting $6.25 paid by the employer, a $0.40 supplement from the EITC for each $1.00 earned ($2.50 total), and a negative $0.08 paid in payroll taxes for each $1.00 earned ($0.48 total). Thus, for workers earning this wage, the EITC encourages additional work up to four-fifths time.

Working just over 32 hours per week, the $6.25 per hour employee reaches the plateau of the EITC program and benefits remain constant. Now this person receives an effective wage of $5.77 per hour, reflecting

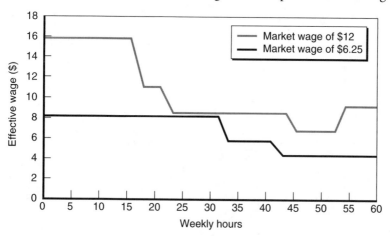

Figure 2.5—Effective Wage after Taxes and Federal EITC Benefits

$6.25 paid by the employer minus deductions for payroll taxes, the same as in the absence of the EITC. In the plateau range, the EITC offers no additional incentive to work but does increase total income for the family. At around 42 hours of work per week, the EITC begins to phase out with benefits being withdrawn at the rate of $0.21 for each $1.00 received in wages. This reduces the worker's effective wage to $4.46 per hour.

The same pattern holds for moderate-wage workers, but the incentive for additional work applies over a much shorter range of hours, because it takes fewer hours of work to hit the thresholds for the EITC. In fact, for moderate-wage families, the current federal EITC program creates appreciable disincentives to moving from half-time to full-time work, with the effective wage dropping by more than a third of its initial value. Figure 2.6 demonstrates how the three sections of the EITC—the phasein, plateau, and phaseout—and the income tax threshold correspond to the steps in the effective wage line for the worker earning $12 per hour. Up to about 15 hours of work per week, the worker effectively earns $15.88 per hour. Such a high wage provides strong encouragement for the worker to engage in part-time work. In contrast, increasing hours to slightly beyond 20 per week—into the phaseout range of the EITC—pays this individual $8.56 per hour, falling nearly

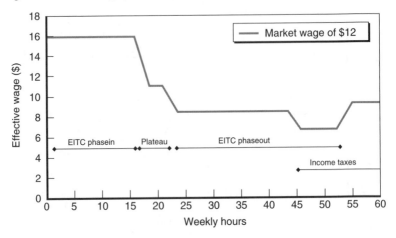

Figure 2.6—Effective Wage for the Moderate-Wage Worker after Taxes and Federal EITC Benefits

$3.50 short of this person's market wage and nearly $2.50 below what this person would earn per hour in the absence of EITC (shown in Figure 2.4). In considering whether to increase hours beyond 44 per week, this person faces a wage of only $6.76 per hour. This not only represents a net wage falling 44 percent below this individual's market wage, it constitutes a 57 percent drop from what this worker earns working part-time.

Greater Work Disincentives for Families on Food Stamps

Any EITC family who also collects Food Stamps encounters enhanced disincentives for working beyond part-time employment. Figure 2.7 plots the effective wages adding Food Stamps benefits in addition to participating in the EITC program. Both workers start out at the same levels as in Figure 2.5 because of the "earnings disregard" feature of Food Stamps, which ignores initial earnings in calculating benefit levels. Thereafter, benefit levels are reduced at a rate of $1 for every $3 earned, thus lowering the disposable income available for each hour worked and the effective wage for these hours. Of course, these families are better off than they would have been without Food Stamps,

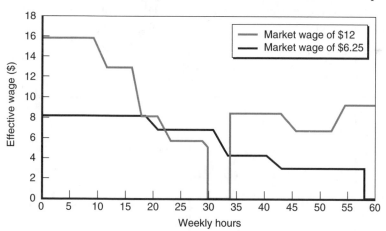

Figure 2.7—Effective Wage after Taxes, Federal EITC Benefits, and Food Stamps

since their disposable income is higher with the payment of benefits. The problem arises because each family receives lower returns to additional work as the Food Stamps structure phases out benefits.

For workers earning $12 per hour, the drop in effective wages is dramatic. To clarify which programs are functioning in each range, Figure 2.8 again maps the effective ranges for the EITC, Food Stamps, and income taxes for the $12 per hour earner. As with just the EITC, the effective wage starts at $15.88 per hour, because the initial earnings are disregarded in the Food Stamps program. However, beginning at about 10 hours of work per week, Food Stamps benefits decline. Once the EITC also begins to phase out, in the 23 to 30 hours per week range, the effective wage plunges to $5.68 per hour. Food Stamps benefits cut off shortly after 30 hours of work per week, when monthly earnings slightly exceed $1,500, yielding a sharp loss in benefits of nearly $24 per week. To make up for this loss, the worker would need to work four extra hours a week. Thus, Figures 2.7 and 2.8 present the effective wage as remaining at zero until enough net earnings accumulate to overcome the full loss of Food Stamps benefits. Above 34 hours per week, wages recover to the after-payroll-tax, after-EITC phaseout level of $8.56 per hour. Continuing from this point, the effective wage eventually falls again slightly beyond 40 hours per week, reflecting the initiation of

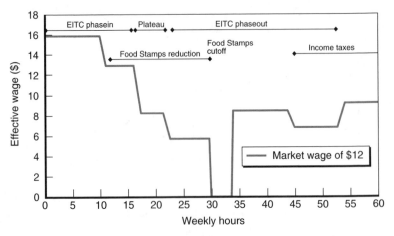

Figure 2.8—Effective Wage for the Moderate-Wage Worker after Taxes, Federal EITC Benefits, and Food Stamps

income taxes; beyond 50 hours, it rises once more because of the end of the EITC. In contemplating whether to move from part-time to full-time employment, the worker in this family earns below $6.00 per hour overall—less than half the wage paid by his or her employer. This amounts to more than a 50 percent implicit tax rate on earnings, which undoubtedly constitutes a substantial work disincentive.

The $6.25 per hour family does not escape these work disincentives either. The tradeoff for the effective wage of $8.27 per hour up to about half-time employment is a decline in the family's effective wage until just beyond 30 hours per week, where it remains at $4.26 until full-time employment. This return for work is $1.50 below the take-home wage this family would earn in the absence of the EITC and Food Stamps program.

California Programs Further Discourage Full-Time Work

Finally, welfare recipients face the strongest adverse incentives to full-time work. The worsened incentives arise from the extra loss of CalWORKs benefits occurring as a family increases its earnings. Figure 2.9 graphs the effective wages for two families when they simultaneously collect CalWORKs benefits, the cash equivalent of Food Stamps, and the federal EITC after paying their federal and state payroll and income

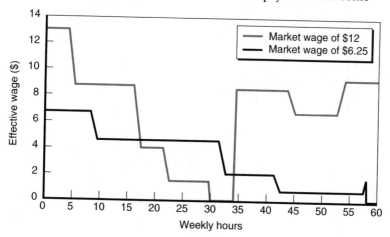

Figure 2.9—Effective Wage after Taxes, Federal EITC Benefits, Food Stamps, and CalWORKs

taxes. After a modest exemption for the first dollars earned attributable to the earnings disregard, every dollar received in wages by the family directly leads to a reduction in their CalWORKs and Food Stamps benefits at a rate of about $2 for every $3 earned. Beyond earnings levels reaching the phaseout range of the federal EITC, disposable income received for each hour worked falls dramatically.

As before, Figure 2.10 isolates the $12 per hour worker family, showing which policies are in effect in each range of the effective wage. Once again, after high initial rewards to work, this $12 per hour worker family experiences substantial work disincentives, although family income is, of course, higher than in the absence of participation. Now the effective wage starts at $13.00 per hour, and beginning at about five hours of work per week, it plunges to approximately $1.50 per hour just beyond 20 hours per week. Food Stamps benefits cut off at approximately 30 hours per week, which Figure 2.10 depicts by setting the effective wage equal to zero until earnings (net of EITC, taxes, and CalWORKs) amass enough to raise disposable income. Slightly before 35 hours per week, the effective wage bounces back to $8.56, reflecting loss of both Food Stamps and CalWORKs eligibility, which increases returns to work because the family no longer suffers a loss of benefits as earnings rise. In contemplating whether to move from part-time to full-

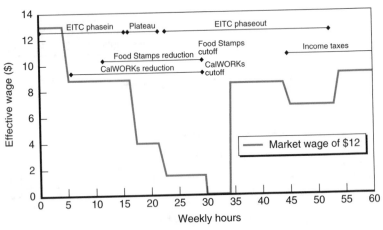

Figure 2.10—Effective Wage for the Moderate-Wage Worker after Taxes, Federal EITC Benefits, Food Stamps, and CalWORKs

time employment, the worker in this family earns, on average, only about $2.25 per hour over the range of 20 to 40 hours per week. This hourly rate represents merely a sixth of this family's gross wage received from the employer, and it falls nearly $9 below the effective wage applicable if the family does not participate in CalWORKs, Food Stamps, or the EITC. Clearly, the returns to work beyond part-time are exceedingly low.

Circumstances are not much brighter for the family supported by a $6.25 per hour job. After earning about $6.77 per hour for the first 10 hours worked per week, the worker's effective wage drops until it reaches just over $2.00 per hour for the last seven hours worked before attaining full-time employment. Once again, the diminished rewards undoubtedly discourage many of these families from working beyond part-time.

3. Policy Alternatives for California

The existing EITC, Food Stamps, and CalWORKs benefit structures provide the backdrop for a California state EITC. If the state EITC is intended to encourage work and direct benefits to poor families, the state must consider design features beyond merely emulating the federal EITC system. This chapter describes four EITC-type programs as alternative policies for a state EITC. In contrast to the current federal system, two of these programs use both earnings and wages to compute a family's benefits. Chapter 4 compares the work incentives of these alternatives.

Supplementing the Federal EITC Program

To date, the main EITC program design considered for California proposes a state program that follows the rules of the current federal EITC and pays benefits as a fixed percentage of the federal amounts. Administrative ease is a key advantage of such an EITC because it does not require any new calculations. For this reason, an "add-on" EITC of this sort has been the most common design adopted by states implementing their own EITCs. In 15 out of 17 states that had implemented state EITCs as of April 2003, the state EITC was typically set between 10 and 25 percent of the federal credit, although five of these states did not make the state EITC refundable.[1] In their deliberations of AB 106 in 2000, California legislators called for a California EITC equal to 15 percent of the federal EITC.

Figure 3.1 presents the benefit structure of a state EITC representing 15 percent of the federal program for families with one and with two or

---

[1] Details about the various state credits can be found in Johnson (1999, 2003).

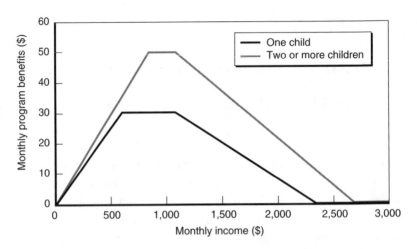

Figure 3.1—Monthly Benefits from a 15 Percent California Add-On to the Federal Earnings-Based EITC Program for Different Family Sizes

more qualifying children, expressed in 2001 dollars.[2] Figure 3.2 shows how these state credits add on to federal benefits for a family with two qualifying children at different levels of monthly earnings. As is clear from these figures, a state EITC that emulates the federal program entails the same three distinct ranges:

- a phasein range where the size of the credit rises with earnings;
- a plateau where additional earnings do not affect the size of the credit; and
- a phaseout range where the credit falls with additional earnings, eventually reaching zero.

In the phasein range, the state EITC offers a credit equal to 6 percent of earnings (15 percent of the federal 40 percent rate) for families with two or more qualified children. In the plateau range, the state credit remains unchanged at its maximum level of $50 per month. During the phaseout range, the credit declines at a rate of 3.15 percent (15 percent

_____

[2]A qualifying child is a biological, adopted, foster or step child, or grandchild who is either under age 19 or under age 24 and a full-time student. The credit has the same basic structure but a higher rate and higher maximum benefit for families with two or more children.

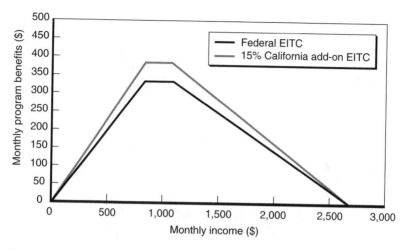

Figure 3.2—Monthly Benefits from a 15 Percent California Add-On to the Federal Earnings-Based EITC Program for a Family with Two Children

of the federal 21 percent rate) for families with two or more children. Thus, the 15 percent add-on state EITC proposed by the California legislature in 2000 would pay $6.00 for every additional $100 of earnings when a two-child family first started working. It also would phase out these benefits at a rate of $3.15 per $100 earned after the family reached a prescribed level of earnings.

EITC Structures Used in Other States

Among the states currently offering earned income tax credits, there are two exceptions to the standard federal add-on EITC strategy. These unusual cases are Indiana and Minnesota, whose EITC benefits (for a family with one child) are compared in Figure 3.3 to an add-on credit set at 15 percent of the federal credit. The Indiana EITC is designed to assist the very poorest families with earnings. It provides the highest benefit, about $35 a month, to families with earnings close to (but greater than) zero. As income rises, the credit is gradually reduced and completely eliminated when earned income reaches slightly more than $1,000 a month. Rather than a straight 15 percent of the federal credit, the Indiana credit provides a higher benefit to very poor working families. On the other hand, it does not encourage additional work because the

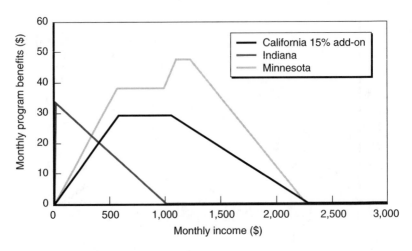

Figure 3.3—Comparison of Monthly Benefits from a 15 Percent California Add-On EITC and EITC Programs in Indiana and Minnesota for a Family with One Child

benefit falls with earnings. Because of this last feature, the Indiana credit is frequently not considered a "true" EITC.

The structure of Minnesota's EITC, called the Working Family Credit (WFC), addresses a problem at the opposite end of the EITC income range. Before 1998, the WFC was set at 15 percent of the federal credit, as proposed for California. Under the rules of Minnesota's welfare program, the combination of declining welfare grants, loss of Food Stamps, payroll taxes, the federal EITC, and the state WFC together resulted in no additional income for families increasing their earnings in the phaseout range. In fact, a full-time working parent receiving a wage increase from $6.00 to $7.00 an hour would actually lose income. A move from $7.00 to $8.00 would provide an income gain of less than $200 annually. To address this "no net gain" problem, the Minnesota legislature reformulated the WFC in 1998, providing a larger state credit to families in this particular part of the income range.[3] The Minnesota line in Figure 3.3 represents this new formulation, where the second step up in the credit helps make work pay for families leaving welfare.

---

[3]Madden (1999).

Low- and High-Earnings State EITCs

An add-on EITC, like the credit most recently proposed for California, targets the same families as the federal EITC, using the same eligibility criteria and same income ranges. However, California need not tie its EITC to the federal version. Like Indiana or Minnesota, the California earned income tax credit could be designed to focus on the needs of families at a certain place in the income distribution. Although such targeted credits could be developed using a variety of structures, we consider two simple cases that help explain the challenges and potential benefits of constructing an EITC less closely tied to the federal rules. To make these alternatives comparable to the current proposal, we have selected as examples credits that hit the same maximum level as the 15 percent federal add-on credit.

Our two alternative structures, pictured in Figure 3.4, are designed to target select portions of the income distribution. The low-earnings option, described by the triangle on the left in Figure 3.4, focuses the credit on the lowest end of the income range covered by the federal EITC. This credit phases in at the same rate and hits the same

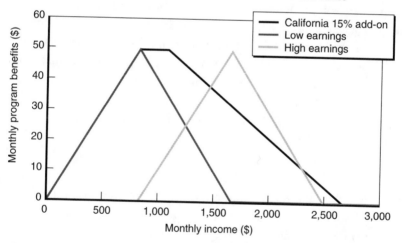

Figure 3.4—Comparison of Monthly Benefits from a 15 Percent California Add-On EITC and High- and Low-Earnings Options for a Family with Two Children

maximum as the 15 percent add-on EITC program. That is, for a family with two children, it is equal to 6 percent of earnings up to a maximum of $50. However, rather than having a plateau, it starts to phase out immediately, at the same 6 percent rate. This option, therefore, keeps the phasein features of the current proposal, augmenting the federal credit only for the lowest-earning families and phasing out entirely as a family approaches the poverty threshold for a family of three.

The high-earnings option, represented by the triangle on the right in Figure 3.4, is identical to the low-earnings option, but applies to a higher income range. Like the low-earnings option, it phases in at 6 percent for a two-child family, hits a maximum of $50, and then immediately phases out at 6 percent. However, families do not become eligible for this credit until they have reached the start of the federal plateau ($840) and the maximum credit occurs beyond the plateau (at just under $1,700). Families lose all state credits by about $2,500 of monthly earnings—an income level lower than the earnings cutoff for the federal credit.

These two alternatives preserve the maximum credit but reduce the range of income eligibility, so both would be significantly less expensive than an add-on proposal. However, our goal in selecting these options is not to suggest less costly alternatives but rather to examine how different structures can change the work incentives and distribution of benefits— the issues we take up in Chapters 4 and 5. Indeed the conceptual issues would be the same if these low-earnings and high-earnings options were set to be equally (or more) generous than the 15 percent add-on. Moreover, more complex alternatives can be constructed by combining low- and high-targeted credit ranges and rates.

A Wage-Based State EITC

The EITC and the minimum wage are commonly seen as two different strategies to target workers supporting families on low wages. In fact, an EITC benefit structure can be designed to adjust for the hourly wage of a worker, capturing attractive components of the EITC (i.e., targeting workers with families) and attractive components of the minimum wage (i.e., targeting workers with low market wages).[4] That is, a wage-based EITC would treat a low-wage worker working full-time differently from a higher-wage worker working half-time, even if their incomes were identical. Consider three families, all with two children and headed by workers earning $6.25, $9.00, and $12.00 per hour. If we define "full-time" as 40 hours per week or 170 hours per month, these family breadwinners would, respectively, earn $1,062, $1,530, and $2,040 working full-time. When it was expanded in 1993, the federal EITC was explicitly designed to fill the gap between minimum-wage work and the poverty threshold, setting the maximum credit threshold at the income attained by working full-time at the minimum wage. In this way, the EITC was targeted with greater concern for the first family than the last. As we have seen, low-wage workers are encouraged by the EITC to work up to full-time, but the $12 per hour worker receives the maximum benefit by working half-time and also faces declining benefits and the disincentives described in the previous chapter by working additional hours.

The wage-based EITC structure we examine would provide the full 15 percent supplement to those working full-time. Those working less than full-time would receive the equivalent of the benefit they would qualify for at full-time work, discounted by their percentage of time worked.[5] In other words, those working half-time would receive half of

---

[4]Instead of basing EITC benefits on earnings and hourly wages, one could develop an equivalent system by making benefits depend on earnings and hours of work. Several welfare programs outside the United States pay benefits based on the number of hours per week a recipient works. Canada's Self-Sufficiency Program provides a large income supplement to those who are low-income and work at least 30 hours a week. The Family Credit program in Great Britain gives a bonus to families when they reach 16 hours per week and another bonus at 30 hours. Obviously, a benefit schedule based on hours of work and earnings is just another way of looking at a program that is based on wages and earnings, because knowing two of the three numbers determines the third (i.e., earnings = wage * hours). We specify our redesigns of the EITC in terms of wages rather than hours because it is not our intention to encourage particular choices for weekly hours of work, and our approach more readily applies to families with more than one earner.

[5]We determine wage as total earnings in the year divided by total hours worked. Hours worked is commonly used in unemployment insurance and should not be difficult to record accurately.

what they would receive working full-time for the same wage under the 15 percent add-on formula. Someone working full-time at $6.25 would receive 15 percent of their federal EITC benefit, the same as in the add-on. The $12 per hour worker would earn $2,040 working full-time, which would qualify for $6 per month ($72 per year). If the worker earned the same wage but only worked half-time, the add-on EITC structure would provide $50 per month, the same as the full-time worker earning $6.25 per hour. The wage-based structure, however, would give the half-time worker half the full-time-equivalent benefit, or $3 per month ($36 per year). The benefit would be higher if more hours were worked. (As with the low-earnings and high-earnings options, this plan would be less expensive overall, but the structure could be adjusted to provide a higher maximum benefit, using the savings from the high-wage workers to provide higher benefits to the low-wage workers at the same cost).

As Figure 3.5 demonstrates, this benefit structure has two key features. First, it provides for different schedules of benefits by income level depending on workers' wages. Second, for moderate- and higher-wage workers, it expands the range of incomes over which the benefits increase (at a lower rate) and shortens the range over which benefits decrease. Each schedule extends in a straight line from $0 to the point

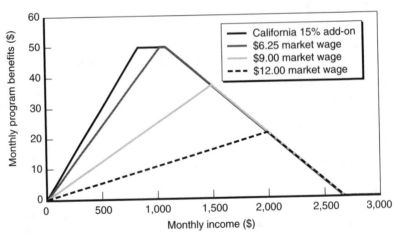

Fiure 3.5—Monthly Benefits from a 15 Percent California Wage-Based EITC Program for a Family with Two Children

on the state earnings-based EITC schedule representing full-time work at a given wage. After full-time work is attained, each schedule reverts to the regular state EITC schedule. A worker earning the minimum wage has an EITC schedule that closely follows the add-on EITC schedule, whereas those with higher wages tend to have flatter benefit schedules up until reaching full-time employment. In this way, this wage-based EITC not only targets the highest benefits to the lowest-wage workers, but it also provides incentives for moving toward full-time work.

Unlike the previous EITC option, this wage-based state EITC design raises two major questions about program design. First, given earnings and hours for couples, how does one determine "the" wage? Second, how does one measure full-time employment when more than one family member works? Our analysis of work incentives abstracts from these complications by focusing on single-parent examples. However, these issues are real for implementation as well as for predicting the distribution of benefits in Chapter 5.

There are two options for addressing how to compute the hourly wage of a family when more than one person works: (1) We could compute wages independently for each worker and assign the highest wage to the family, or (2) we could divide total family earnings by total hours worked by all members to compute a wage averaged across members. Using the maximum wage makes sense because we are trying to encourage the person receiving that wage to work (because he or she has the highest marginal productivity), and thus we should tie incentives to his or her wage.[6] On the other hand, using an average wage is perhaps more straightforward because it treats the joint tax filers as one economic unit. This approach also seems less prone to "marriage penalty" problems, which would occur if a couple experienced a lower credit as a unit than would occur if each of the two people were treated as single individuals. Together, these characteristics make the second approach our choice in the distributional calculations.[7]

---

[6] In other words, the work efforts of the person with the highest wage result in the highest output for a given set of inputs.

[7] We experimented with both methods, and the distributional results presented are not sensitive to the approach selected.

Turning to the second complication, what is meant by full-time hours for a family with multiple persons employed? The answer depends on whether policymakers want to encourage joint filers to both work full-time or to allow incentive effects to drop off after one person is working full-time. In our analyses of alternative EITC programs, we assume that hours worked by the couple above the equivalent of one full-time worker are subject to the same phaseouts as under the current EITC system. Alternatively, we could have provided for a plateau from 2,000 annual hours (full-time for one person) out to some additional amount that could be as high as 4,000 hours. Although benefits would not grow, work would not be discouraged. Naturally, this would make a program more expensive depending on how many people are affected, although fewer families with two full-time workers participate in the EITC program than single-parent families.

A Wage-Subsidy State EITC

Another approach for developing a benefit schedule is simply to give families with children a wage subsidy equivalent to the difference between their market wage and some predetermined threshold. Under a wage-subsidy EITC, the credit is highest for the lowest-wage workers, with workers earning wages above the threshold receiving no state credit. Although this program is clearly modeled after the minimum wage, it differs in two important respects. First, it supports only those who have dependent children and are poor. Second, it is financed through state tax revenue. This means that funding comes from the progressive income tax rather than from the regulated method of the minimum wage, where poor families are likely to pay a disproportionate share of the costs, through higher prices on goods produced with minimum-wage labor.[8] Furthermore, this wage subsidy will not discourage businesses from hiring low-skill workers in the way that many argue a minimum wage does.

Figure 3.6 illustrates a credit with a threshold of $7.50 for every hour worked, up to full-time. A minimum-wage worker supporting children

---

[8]See O'Brien-Strain and MaCurdy (2000) for further discussion of who pays for minimum wage increases.

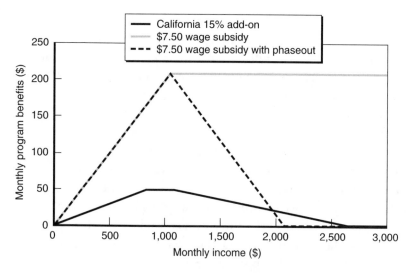

Figure 3.6—Monthly Benefits from a 15 Percent California Wage-Subsidy
EITC Program for a Family Working for $6.25 per Hour
with Two Children

would get a credit or subsidy of $1.25 (equal to $7.50 minus $6.25) for
each hour worked under the full-time maximum; the $12 per hour
worker would receive no state credit. Figure 3.6 shows two options for
the benefit schedule. The solid lines presume that benefits for workers
working beyond full-time are phased out at the same rate as assumed in
the add-on option. The dashed lines, on the other hand, build in no
phaseout of benefits; the worker keeps the tax credits earned at full-time
employment, with benefits taxed away only through the regular income
tax program. (Alternatively, benefits could plateau for a range of
earnings before declining with various benefit-reduction rates.) To
reflect the family size adjustments in the existing EITC, the threshold
wage could also vary with family size. In this way, the wage-subsidy
EITC can essentially set different "minimum wages" for different size
families.

The EITC approach differs from a direct wage subsidy in that it
maintains a close link to total family earnings and to the presence of
children; it would also be administered through the tax system rather
than by employers. These features help reduce, but do not entirely
eliminate, other potential incentive problems associated with a wage

subsidy. In particular, a wage subsidy gives workers earning less than the threshold wage no incentive to seek higher-paying jobs. In addition, these workers would have little incentive to undertake training leading to incremental wage increases because they would obtain no benefits from such wage changes. Moreover, employers might be tempted to lower the wages of their workers supporting low-income families with children because government credits would make up the difference. To mitigate these potential adverse incentives, one could design a wage-subsidy EITC raising a person's wage only partially to the prescribed level. For example, a wage-subsidy EITC might pay a credit equal to 50 or 75 percent of the difference between the worker's wage and the established threshold level. In such a program, a worker would always benefit from receiving a higher market wage and, thus, would take advantage of better-paying employment opportunities.

4. Options for Improving Work Incentives

In this chapter, we assess the effects of our alternative EITC designs on the work incentives created by existing EITC and public assistance policies in California. For each of the options presented in Chapter 3, we examine the change in effective wages for two-child families supported by single parents earning $6.25 and $12 per hour. We consider two scenarios: families receiving EITC but no other benefits and families receiving CalWORKs along with Food Stamps. Finally, the analysis also compares the effects of the state EITC proposals to the work incentives created by increases of the minimum wage.

An Add-On EITC Exacerbates Work Disincentives

Figures 4.1 and 4.2 demonstrate how introducing a 15 percent add-on state EITC alters the effective wages of two single-parent two-child families: one earning $6.25 per hour and another earning $12 per hour. These are the same single-parent two-child families considered in the previous chapters. Figure 4.1 presents the change in work incentives for a working family that does not rely on any public assistance during the year, which we will refer to as a "non-aided family." Figure 4.2 shows the changes in the effective wages earned by a family who collects Food Stamps and CalWORKS benefits in addition to the federal EITC, which we refer to as a "welfare-recipient family."

As Figure 4.1 shows, shifts in the effective wages induced by a California supplement to the EITC are quite small. For the $12 per hour non-aided family, the increase amounts to about $0.60 per hour, from $15.88 per hour to $16.60 per hour, for less than 16 hours worked per week. Beyond part-time employment, the effective wage declines by $0.38 per hour, from $8.56 per hour to $8.18 per hour. For the $6.25 per hour family, effective wages rise by $0.38 per hour at low levels of

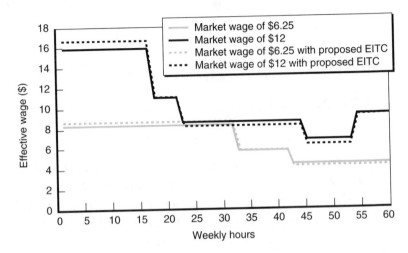

Figure 4.1—Effective Wage with a 15 Percent California Add-On EITC

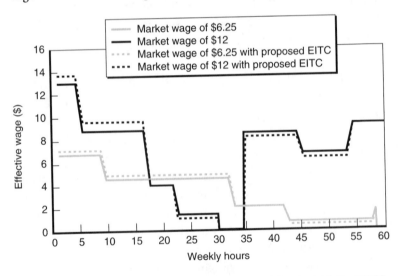

Figure 4.2—Effective Wage with a 15 Percent California Add-On EITC, Food Stamps, and CalWORKs

earnings, from $8.27 per hour to $8.65 per hour, and fall by less than $0.20 per hour after reaching full-time employment. Thus, the state supplementary EITC barely changes effective wages and work incentives for non-aided families.

To the degree that it does have an effect, a 15 percent California supplement to the federal EITC enhances work incentives at the lowest earnings levels for non-aided working poor families and worsens incentives at higher levels. Consequently, families are further encouraged with the introduction of the state EITC to work part-time rather than to not work at all, but they are further discouraged from moving from part-time to full-time work.

For welfare-recipient families (Figure 4.2), the story is similar. The 15 percent California supplement to the federal EITC helps promote work at the lowest earnings levels and discourages work at higher levels. For the $12 per hour family, returns from work go up by $0.72 per hour for up to 20 hours per week, and returns fall by as much as $0.38 per hour for hours beyond part-time. For the $6.25 per hour family, effective wages rise by $0.38 per hour for hours worked up to full-time employment.

For moderate-wage families who could move off welfare by working full-time, the disincentive effects of the add-on state EITC further reduce the attractiveness of moving from part-time employment to a work schedule that would lead to self-sufficiency. A $12 per hour family loses welfare eligibility at around 31 hours of work per week. Thus, a breadwinner in such family who is working part-time at 20 hours per week must increase his or her effort by 12 hours to leave the CalWORKs rolls. Yet the return for these extra hours drops from $1.48 per hour to $1.10 per hour with adoption of the 15 percent state supplement to the EITC.

Low- and High-Earnings EITCs Slightly Improve Incentives

Where an add-on EITC merely amplifies the work incentives inherent in the federal program, the low-earnings and high-earnings programs amplify the federal EITC in some ranges and offset it in other ranges. The low-earnings EITC (Figures 4.3 and 4.4) encourages work effort at low levels of earnings—just like the supplemental EITC—but generally discourages work in the midrange of earnings with its more rapid phaseout, leaving the incentives at higher ranges of work unaffected

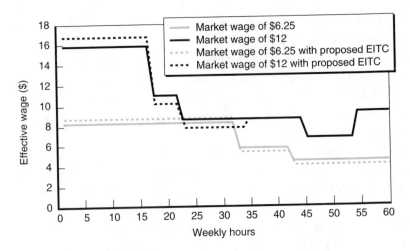

Figure 4.3—Effective Wage with a Low-Earnings EITC

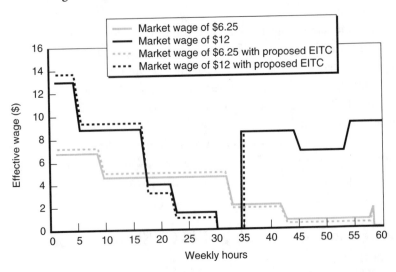

Figure 4.4—Effective Wage with a Low-Earnings EITC, Food Stamps, and CalWORKs

relative to no state EITC. The low-earnings option targets the state EITC toward low-wage earners and away from moderate-wage earners. A $12 per hour family has lower rewards from work in the midrange of hours (because the state EITC is phasing out) and improved incentives at higher levels, where there is no state EITC. Work incentives are increased over a longer range for the low-wage worker. Work incentives for the $6.25 per hour family improve slightly from the no state EITC option up to about 30 hours per week and worsen thereafter.

In contrast, the high-earnings EITC targets the EITC toward moderate-wage workers (Figures 4.5 and 4.6). It does not alter work incentives at low levels of earnings. Instead, it encourages work effort in the range of $800 to $1,600 per month. As it phases out, it discourages additional work activities between $1,600 and $2,400 per month. Consequently, this state EITC leaves incentives unaffected at the lowest hours. For the $12 per hour worker, rewards from work rise to encourage part-time employment and then fall just before full-time employment. For the $6.25 per hour family, work incentives are slightly improved after 30 hours per week, with this effect persisting well beyond full-time employment.

Turning to welfare-recipient families, the high-earnings state EITC offers a decided advantage over the low-earnings program in encouraging employed families to achieve self-sufficiency from CalWORKs. The low-earnings EITC program (Figure 4.4) further discourages employed welfare families from leaving the CalWORKs rolls, whereas the high-earnings option (Figure 4.6) strictly increases rewards from work at the boundary between poverty and above-poverty earnings. It is exactly in this range of earnings where extra work effort moves a family off the

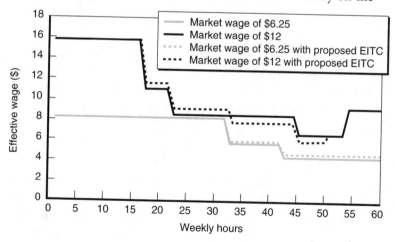

Figure 4.5—Effective Wage with a High-Earnings EITC

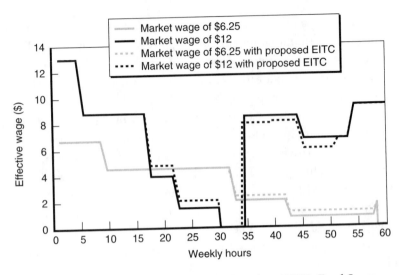

Figure 4.6—Effective Wage with a High-Earnings EITC, Food Stamps, and CalWORKs

CalWORKs caseload. For a $12 per hour family working part-time and considering increasing its hours enough to exit from CalWORKs, introduction of the low-earnings option drops its effective wage from $1.48 to $0.76; adoption of the high-earnings option raises this hourly wage from $1.48 to $2.20. For the $6.25 per hour CalWORKs family, the low-earnings state EITC decreases its effective wage from $0.77 to $0.40 as earnings near the level prompting an exit from the welfare rolls; the high-earnings EITC increases this hourly wage from $0.77 to $1.15.

Consequently, among the three earnings-based state EITC options, only the high-earnings program enhances rewards from work for families with earnings near the poverty level. The add-on and low-earnings EITCs provide the largest incentives for families to raise work hours when their annual earnings range between $0 and $10,000. For non-aided families, distinctions in these work incentives may not be sufficiently different to suggest preference for one EITC structure over the other. For aided families, however, CalWORKs, Food Stamps, and the federal EITC combine to create substantial disincentives to increasing hours of work, inducing implicit tax rates exceeding 90 percent for hours leading to exit from the CalWORKs program. When faced with this implicit rate, families raise their disposable income by less than $1 for every $10 of earnings. Clearly, a state EITC offsetting this weak return to work should be attractive to policymakers. Only the high-earnings EITC achieves this offset, albeit the reduction in this implicit tax rate reaches only a modest 6 percent. Of course, if policymakers were to use the savings in cost over the add-on EITC, they could further reduce the implicit tax rate.

Mitigating Work Disincentives through a Wage-Based State EITC

One can overcome many of the adverse consequences of earnings-based EITCs on work incentives by revising these programs to incorporate features of the wage-based EITC program. The wage-based EITC (Figures 4.7 and 4.8) improves work incentives for all families up to full-time employment. For the non-aided $12 per hour family depicted in Figure 4.7, the worker earns just slightly more (about $0.10) than he or she would receive in the absence of a state EITC for hours up to full-time employment. Because it is designed to encourage full-time work, the effective wage beyond full-time employment for the $12 per hour worker falls to a level about $0.40 lower than the wage without a state EITC. Thus, between 40 and 53 hours of work, the phaseout of

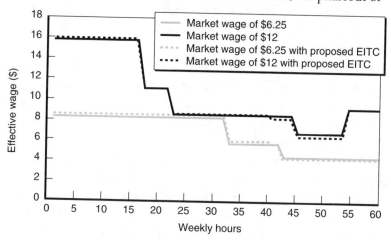

Figure 4.7—Effective Wage with a Wage-Based EITC

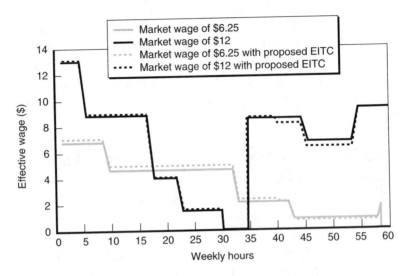

Figure 4.8—Effective Wage with a Wage-Based EITC, Food Stamps, and CalWORKs

this EITC creates additional work disincentives for the $12 per hour worker.

For all hours up to full-time employment, a family supported by a $6.25 per hour worker gains considerably more from the wage-based state EITC than its higher-wage counterpart. For hours up to about 40 per week, this worker earns $0.30 more per hour than without a state EITC. After 30 hours, the federal EITC begins to phase out, dropping the effective wage from $8.57 to approximately $6.10, still $0.30 higher than without the wage-based EITC. Shortly after reaching full-time employment, the state EITC benefits also begin to phase out, leading to an effective wage of $4.26, now nearly $0.20 below that applicable in the federal-only EITC regime.

The wage-based state EITC also mitigates the adverse effects of welfare and taxes on additional hours of work. As with all the EITC options, the pattern of benefits is the same for welfare families as it is for non-aided families, but as Figure 4.8 shows, the benefits of this EITC option continue to accrue for all workers up to full-time employment, including in the ranges with the highest disincentives for moderate-wage workers. If policymakers wished to encourage work beyond 40 hours for any of the workers considered above—for example, to mitigate the disincentives from the phaseout of Food Stamps—then they could do so by shifting the phaseout range of the wage-based EITC to begin at a higher number of hours or by introducing a gentler reduction of benefits.

Wage-Subsidy State EITC Further Improves Incentives

As we saw in the previous chapter, the wage-subsidy EITC benefits only the $6.25 per hour worker because it provides a credit only to workers earning less than $7.50 per hour. Figures 4.9 and 4.10 plot effective wages under this option for the $6.25 per hour worker with and without CalWORKs. In addition to the market wage without a state EITC, each figure shows two versions of the state wage-subsidy EITC: first without any phaseout of benefits and then with a phaseout starting after a worker has reached full employment.

The $7.50 per hour wage-subsidy state EITC raises the effective wage for a $6.25 per hour worker by $1.25 for all hours up to full-time work. This option is thus the strongest strategy for encouraging additional hours of work for low-wage workers. For the non-aided family, this brings the effective wage (after federal EITC) to $9.52 per hour. After 40 hours per week, the no-phaseout version of the EITC

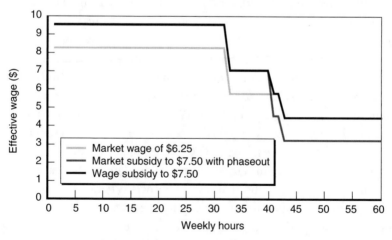

Figure 4.9—Effective Wage with a Wage-Subsidy EITC of $7.50

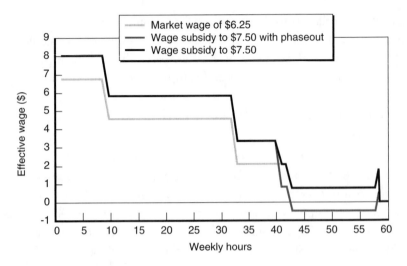

Figure 4.10—Effective Wage with a Wage-Subsidy EITC or Minimum Wage
of $7.50, Food Stamps, and CalWORKs

simply yields an effective wage equal to what it would be in the absence
of a state program. In contrast, the phaseout variant renders a
substantially lower return to work than would occur without a state
EITC until the exhaustion of benefits. For the non-aided family, this
phaseout decreases returns to more than full-time work from $4.46 per
hour (the effective wage without a state EITC) to $3.21 per hour. For
the CalWORKs family, returns fall from $0.77 per hour to –$0.47 per
hour, meaning that workers in these families actually would see their
disposable income decline if they worked beyond 40 hours per week.

In evaluating the work incentives created by the wage-subsidy EITC,
a natural question is how does it compare to an increase in the state
minimum wage? Figures 4.11 and 4.12 make this comparison by
plotting the effective wages implied by a minimum wage of $7.50 in
comparison to the wage-subsidy EITC. For hours up to part-time
employment, a minimum wage offers non-aided families better work
incentives than a wage-subsidy EITC. This occurs because the increased
earnings from a minimum wage qualify for the federal EITC, adding
approximately $0.50 per hour more. At the same time, effective earnings
under the minimum wage fall substantially below those of the wage-
subsidy EITC starting just before full employment. Families with

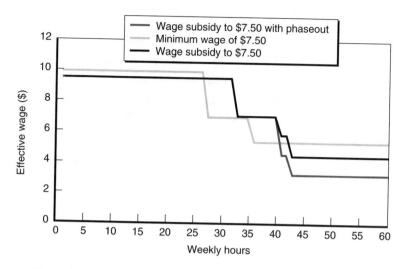

Figure 4.11—Effective Wage with a Wage-Subsidy EITC or Minimum Wage of $7.50

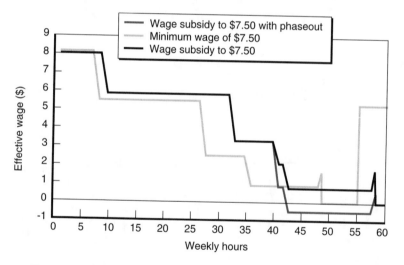

Figure 4.12—Effective Wage with a Wage-Subsidy EITC or Minimum Wage of $7.50, Food Stamps, and CalWORKs

earnings in this range encounter the plateau and then the phaseout ranges on the federal EITC benefit schedule. Beyond full-time work, the minimum wage again achieves an advantage because the wage-subsidy EITC turns off.

For CalWORKs families, the work incentives of the wage-subsidy EITC generally dominate those of a minimum wage for all hours up to full-time employment. The reason is simple. Families see their Food Stamps and CalWORKs benefits fall as their earnings rise until they lose program eligibility. Although earnings from the minimum wage contribute to this taxing away of benefits, income received from a wage-subsidy EITC does not.

5. Level and Share of Benefits Going to Working Poor Families

Other criteria for evaluating EITC options, in addition to encouraging families to work, are the level of benefits families receive and the ability to target the pool of benefits to the intended population. In the case of the EITC, the intended population is generally working families with children and the lowest incomes and, in particular, families supported by low-wage earnings. Obviously the alternative EITC options have significant effects on how much a family receives in benefits. This chapter presents estimates of the benefits families in California actually would receive, given their family structure, wages, and employment patterns, based on simulations from household survey data for California families in 1999. From these estimates of family benefits, we then estimate the total cost of each option described in Chapter 3 and analyze the distribution of benefits across different family types for each option.

Simulating the Allocation of Benefits across Families

We simulate the allocation of EITC benefits using the 1999 waves of the 1996 SIPP, which constitute the most recent available data. The SIPP is a nationally representative survey of households conducted by the U.S. Census Bureau, reporting information on households, families, and individuals over age 15. The survey started in 1996 and collected longitudinal data on families every four months until 2000. The California portion of this survey constitutes a representative sample of California families. It includes monthly data on income and earnings by source, wages, hours worked, demographic characteristics, family structure, and public assistance program participation. This dataset allows us to identify low-income families and low-wage family members. Moreover, it offers sufficient information to simulate the eligibility and distribution of benefits under alternative tax-credit scenarios as well as to assign benefits to families from a hypothetical minimum-wage increase. All quantities are translated into 2001 dollars.

For each state EITC option, our analysis exploits SIPP data to simulate the number of families eligible for the program and the additional income each family would receive under this option, assuming no change in a family's hours of work.[1] Each family is assigned an "average wage" by dividing its total earnings by total hours of work.[2] Using this average wage along with information about a family's income and structure, we calculate the family's tax liability, EITC eligibility, and EITC benefit level. Summing the benefits over all potential taxpaying units within the family yields the family's total EITC benefit level. These benefit levels are then summarized by family structure. Because we do not separate out "subfamilies," families may contain more than one tax filer—such as an adult daughter living with her child and her parents—and the combined family income may exceed the threshold for the EITC but still contain a tax filer who does qualify for the EITC. Consequently, families at all points in the income distribution may receive EITC benefits. Detailed tables on the distribution of benefits are provided in the appendix; key results are summarized below.

Distribution of Benefits to Poor and Near-Poor Families with Children Under Age 18

More families with children would receive a state EITC benefit from the add-on EITC than would receive such a benefit from any of the other EITC alternatives proposed. Figure 5.1 compares the share of California families with children under age 18 who would be eligible for a state EITC benefit under each of the options described in Chapter 3.

---

[1]We assume that there is no change in an individual's work effort in response to the state EITC. This is clearly an abstraction from reality but is implemented for simplicity and to avoid making difficult predictions on this issue.

[2]In this way, couples filing jointly are given a single wage based on their combined earnings divided by their combined hours worked.

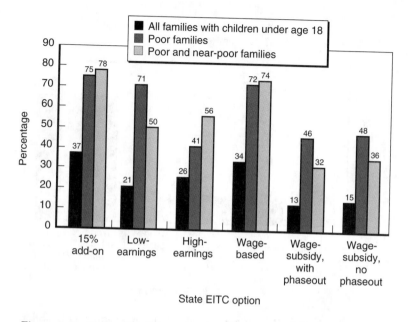

Figure 5.1—Share of California Families with Children Under Age 18
Eligible for Benefits

The wage-based EITC option is closest to the add-on in the share of all families with children, poor families, and near-poor families eligible for benefits. For both the add-on and the wage-based EITC, over one-third of all families with children and about three-fourths of poor and near-poor families would be eligible for an EITC benefit. Because they cover a narrower earnings range, the low- and high-earnings EITCs both provide benefits to a narrower group of families, although the low-earnings EITC serves nearly as many poor families. Not surprisingly, the wage-subsidy EITCs serve the smallest share of families, as only families with low wages qualify, whereas families with higher wages and relatively few work hours may qualify under the other options. Each of the wage-subsidy versions effectively serves primarily poor families, with just under half of the poor families with children including a worker earning less than $7.50 per hour, the threshold wage in this option.

For those families who receive a benefit, however, the wage-subsidy EITC is by far the most generous (Figure 5.2). The average benefit for poor families under the wage-subsidy EITC without a phaseout provision

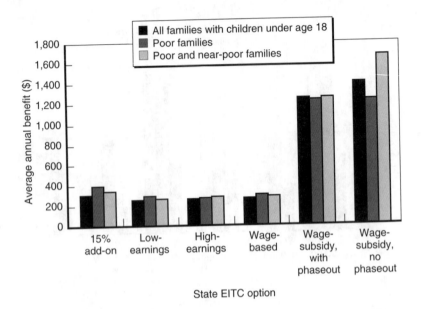

Figure 5.2—Average Benefit per Eligible California Family with Children

is $1,288 annually; near-poor families receive even more on average. In comparison, annual benefits fall just below $300 for the low-earnings, high-earnings, and wage-based EITCs and just below $400 for the add-on EITC.

Under each option presented, virtually all benefits go to families with children under age 18. The remainder goes to very low earners without children and to families with dependent children over age 18. About 80 percent of all the dollars allocated under these EITC plans go to poor and near-poor families with children (Figure 5.3). However, only the low-earnings and wage-subsidy with phaseout ETICs direct the majority of the benefits to poor families. As expected, the high-earnings EITC spends the smallest share of dollars on poor families.

Distribution of Benefits, by Average Wages

The EITC is targeted to low-income families with children, but the different options have strongly different implications for how they treat families supported by low-wage or moderate-wage workers. Figures 5.4 through 5.6 mirror the previous three figures but compare families with

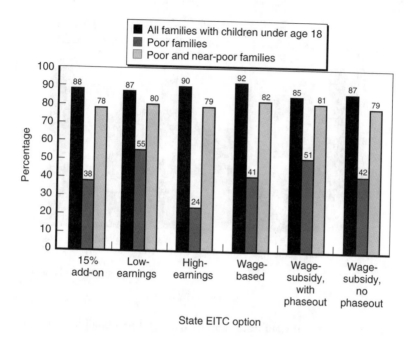

Figure 5.3—Share of State EITC Benefits Provided to Families with Children

average wages below $7.00 (in 2001 dollars) per hour to families with wages between $9 and $12 per hour. Comparisons for additional ranges of wages are presented in the appendix tables.

Under each option, low-wage families are more likely than moderate-wage families to benefit from the state EITC, but the options vary dramatically on the size of the difference in eligibility rates between the two groups. About 90 percent of low-wage families receive some benefits under the 15 percent add-on, the wage-based EITC, and the wage-subsidy EITC with no phaseout. However, only 3 percent of moderate-wage families receive any benefits under the wage-subsidy EITC (and then only because a separate tax filer within the family has a low wage). In contrast, 64 percent of moderate-wage families benefit from the add-on or the wage-based EITC. The low-earnings and high-earnings EITCs represent middle-range cases in terms of the share of moderate-wage families receiving benefits.

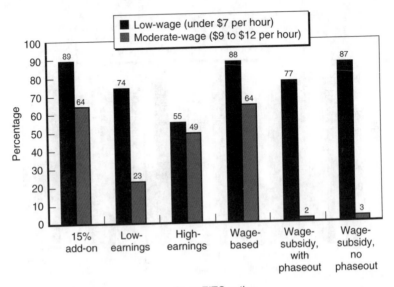

Figure 5.4—Share of California Families with Children Eligible for Benefits, by Average Wage

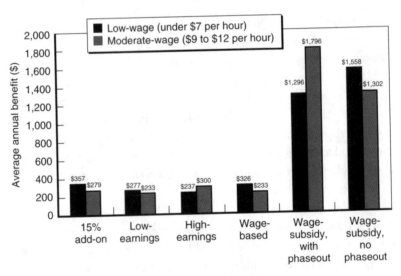

Figure 5.5—Average Benefit per Eligible California Family with Children, by Average Wage

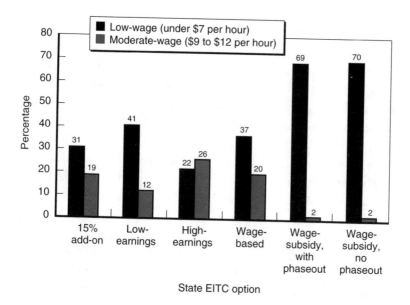

Figure 5.6—Share of State EITC Benefits Provided to Families with Children, by Average Wage

In most cases, moderate-wage families have lower average benefits than low-wage families, by $50 to $100 annually as seen in Figure 5.5. (The high benefits for moderate-wage families under the wage-subsidy option are driven by the presence of low-wage subfamilies, so this distinction is a fluke of family structure rather than the option's design.) The exception is the high-earnings EITC, which pays 27 percent higher benefits on average to moderate-wage families—a predictable outcome following from the focus on higher earnings.

Although 75 to 90 percent of low-wage families benefit under most of the EITC options, only the wage-subsidy EITCs provide benefits primarily to low-wage families. In fact, Figure 5.6 shows that the 15 percent add-on EITC provides only 31 percent of its benefits to low-wage families. The low-earnings and wage-based EITCs each perform better on targeting dollars to low-wage families, although they fall far short of the wage-subsidy versions.

Distribution of Benefits, by Hours Worked

Chapter 4 focused on the incentive effects of the different EITC options in encouraging families to work additional hours, especially in moving from part-time to full-time work. Figures 5.7 through 5.9 compare families working one-quarter to one-half time (500 to 1,000 hours annually) to families working more than half-time but no more than full-time (1,000 to 2,000 hours annually) and families working full-time or more (above 2,000 hours). The last type of family typically has multiple earners in the household. Eighty percent of all families with children in California work more than 2,000 hours annually.

For all options other than the high-earnings EITC, families working 500 to 1,000 hours annually are more likely to benefit from the EITC than are families working more hours (Figure 5.7). Families working more than 2,000 hours annually are by far the least likely to benefit from a state EITC because relatively few families working this many hours fall into the low-income category. The wage-subsidy EITCs are more likely to benefit workers working fewer hours merely because those working

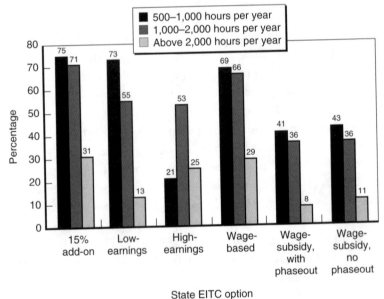

Figure 5.7—Share of California Families with Children Eligible for Benefits, by Annual Hours Worked

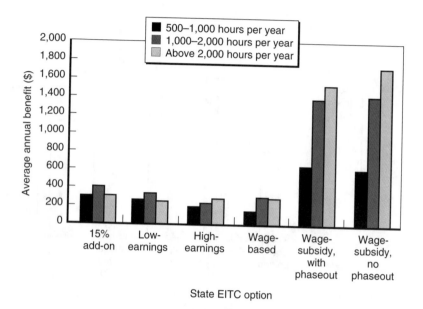

Figure 5.8—Average Benefit per Eligible California Family with
Children, by Annual Hours Worked

shorter schedules are more likely to receive low wages. For the other
options, the difference is driven primarily by the link between low work
hours and low earnings.

Although families working more hours are less likely to receive any
benefits, working longer hours is associated with higher EITC benefits, as
seen in Figure 5.8. This effect is especially strong under the wage-linked
options, where the average benefit to those working more than half-time
is at least double the benefit to those working fewer hours. In this way,
the wage-subsidy EITCs pay the highest benefits to low-wage earners
working more than half-time. Figure 5.9 shows that most of the EITC
dollars go to families working more than 2,000 hours per year because of
the large share of working families with children as well as their relatively
higher levels of benefits. However, 10 to 18 percent of benefits go to
families working less than 500 hours per year (the missing group in the
figure). The high-earnings and wage-based options pay the fewest
benefits to families working fewer than 500 hours per year.

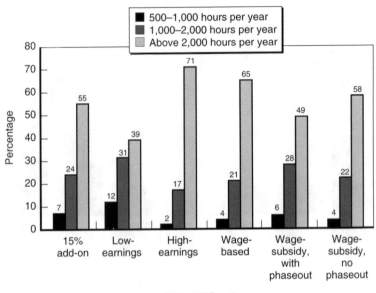

Figure 5.9—Share of State EITC Benefits Provided to Families with Children, by Annual Hours Worked

Distribution of Benefits to CalWORKs Families

The final group of families we consider is CalWORKs families, the group facing the most significant disincentives to full-time work in the existing programs. Figures 5.10 to 5.12 present the share of CalWORKs families eligible for benefits, the average benefits per eligible family, and the share of all benefits going to CalWORKs families. We review the results for poor families as a comparison.

CalWORKs families represent 6 percent of all California families and 15 percent of all California families with children younger than age 18. In comparison, 7 percent of all families are poor. Not all CalWORKs families are poor, as we capture in our family definition additional household members who may not be included in the CalWORKs grant and who may have additional earnings. CalWORKs families are 12 to 20 percentage points less likely than other poor families to benefit from any EITC because fewer of these families are employed.

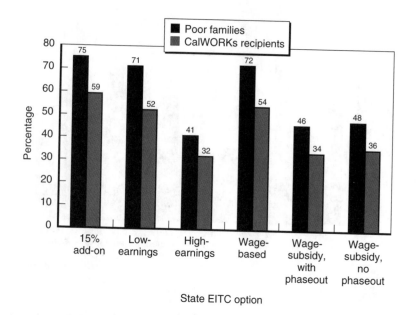

Figure 5.10—Share of Low-Income Families with Children Eligible
for Benefits

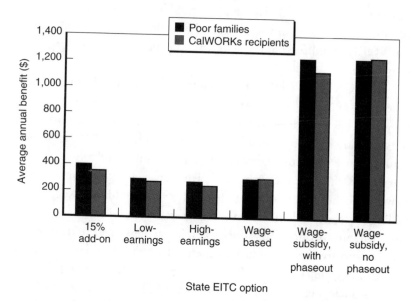

Figure 5.11—Average Benefit per Eligible Low-Income California Family
with Children

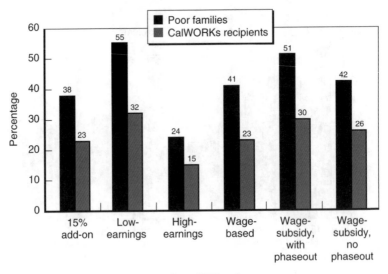

Figure 5.12—Share of State EITC Benefits Provided to Low-Income Families
with Children

Just over half of CalWORKs families would benefit from the 15 percent
add-on, low-earnings, or wage-based EITC options. About one-third of
CalWORKs families would benefit from the high-earnings or wage-
subsidy options.

CalWORKs families are also eligible for lower annual benefits than
other poor families under most of the EITC options, indicating
somewhat lower work effort for these families. The only exception is the
wage-subsidy EITC with no phaseout, under which CalWORKs families
would receive a slightly higher benefit. This result could arise if
CalWORKs households are more likely to have additional workers (who
may not be included in the grant unit) also working for low wages, often
adding up to a total family work effort greater than full-time
employment. Because CalWORKs families are less likely to qualify for
benefits and are eligible for lower benefits than poor families, their share
of total EITC dollars is 15 to 20 percentage points lower than poor
families' analogous share. The low-earnings EITC and wage-subsidy
EITC with phaseout provide the largest share of benefits to CalWORKs
families.

Cost Comparison of EITC Options

Our simulations using SIPP show that the annual cost of the 15 percent add-on EITC would be approximately $732 million, exclusive of any administrative costs. Because the add-on EITC is directly linked to the federal EITC, it is possible to develop cost estimates by taking a simple percentage of federal EITC dollars paid to California taxpayers. Our estimate is higher than such estimates calculated from the costs of the federal EITC because it assumes full participation.[3] In this way, it represents a maximum liability. However, our estimation procedure allows us to create consistent cost comparisons across our different options, as shown in Table 5.1.[4]

As defined in our analysis, all variants of the EITC except for the wage-subsidy versions are less expensive than the add-on EITC. This is an artifact of our setting the maximum rates under each of the non-wage-subsidy options equivalent to the maximum for the add-on EITC. Because the low- and high-earnings EITCs are applicable over narrower ranges of incomes and the wage-based EITC adjusts for hours of work, each of these is necessarily less expensive than the add-on option.

Table 5.1

Estimated Costs of State EITC Options for California

Option for State EITC	Annual Costs (millions, 2001 $)
15 percent add-on to federal EITC	732
Low-earnings	358
High-arnings	427
Wage-based	570
Wage-subsidy to $7.50, no phaseout	1,408
Wage-subsidy to $7.50, with phaseout	1,063

---

[3]See for example, the Assembly Committee on Appropriations analysis of AB 106, available at http://info.sen.ca.gov/pub/01-02/bill/asm/ab_0101-0150/ab_106_cfa_20010507_154031_asm_comm.html, which estimated a benefit cost of $605 million for 2001–2002. Estimates from the Center on Budget and Policy Priorities follow the same approach and yield similar results.

[4]Cost estimates are based on a refundable credit and do not include fraud or administrative costs.

(Depending on how the options are implemented, administrative costs for these other options may be higher.) However, if policymakers selected one of these alternative designs, they could raise the maximum benefit so that families qualifying for the maximum under these EITCs receive more than they would under an add-on EITC, trading off higher benefits for these families with lower benefits for non-targeted families at the same cost as the initial add-on EITC.

Because it pays significantly higher benefits per family, the wage-subsidy EITC is substantially more expensive than the other EITC options, although this is mitigated when a phaseout condition is imposed. In the final section of this chapter, we compare the wage-subsidy options to the minimum wage, which they most resemble.

Effects of a Minimum-Wage Increase Compared to a Wage Subsidy

In contemplating a wage-subsidy EITC to $7.50 per hour, policymakers may ask why they should not simply impose a comparable minimum-wage increase. Despite the apparently similar outcomes, the costs and distributional effects differ, although the most obvious difference is in the payment mechanism. The calculations in Table 5.1 assumed a minimum wage of $6.25, the minimum in effect in 2001. However, because the minimum wage increased to $6.75 in 2002, our comparison of the minimum-wage and wage-subsidy EITC will focus on an incremental increase from $6.75 to $7.50. Our method for calculating the minimum-wage costs and benefits is described in the appendix.

There are two key differences between a wage-subsidy EITC and a minimum wage for raising earnings of low-wage workers supporting families: (1) the targeting of benefits to low-income families with children, and (2) the financing mechanism. Table 5.2 provides comparisons to understand the targeting of benefits; Table 5.3 explores the financing issues.

A wage-subsidy EITC would be far more effective than a minimum-wage increase in targeting benefits to poor and near-poor families. Table 5.2 shows the share of all after-tax, after-federal-EITC benefits going to

Table 5.2

Percentage of Minimum-Wage and Wage-Subsidy Benefits Going to Selected Families Given $7.50 Wage Threshold

	Wage Subsidy, No Phaseout	Wage Subsidy, with Phaseout	Minimum-Wage Increase
Families with children under age 18	88	86	60
With income below poverty	42	50	13
With income below twice poverty	80	82	35
With 50% of earnings from jobs			
Paying below $7 per hour	68	68	27
Paying above $12 per hour	0	1	14
Receiving public assistance	32	36	14

Table 5.3

Benefits and Costs of Wage Subsidy or Minimum Wage of $7.50 (Over and Above the Minimum Wage of $6.75)

	Policy Option ($ millions)		
	Wage Subsidy, No Phaseout	Wage Subsidy, with Phaseout	Minimum-Wage Increase
Benefits to recipients	953	750	2,930
Cost to taxpayers	953	750	−712
Cost to consumers and businesses			3,642

selected groups of families with children younger than age 18. Under the wage-subsidy EITC, all benefits go to families with qualifying children, and almost 90 percent of the benefits go to families with children under age 18. Only 60 percent of minimum-wage benefits would go to such families. If the wage-subsidy EITC includes a phaseout provision, half of all benefits go to families in poverty; more non-poor families benefit if there is no phaseout. In contrast, only a small fraction—13 percent—of the minimum-wage benefits goes to families with children in poverty. This is because relatively few minimum-wage workers support dependents, and minimum-wage workers in families with children are often part of higher-wage households. The wage-subsidy EITC generally does not provide support in these cases, but the minimum wage does not distinguish.

Broadening the low-income perspective to include the near poor captures about one-third of the benefits of a minimum wage; a wage-subsidy EITC would pay four-fifths of the benefits to poor and near-poor families with children. Only 14 percent of minimum-wage benefits would go to families supporting children with CalWORKs, Supplemental Security Income (SSI), or Food Stamps assistance—less than half the share under wage-subsidy EITCs.

The difference in the share of benefits going to the poor is determined largely by whether a program benefits low-wage earners in the same households as higher-wage earners. All low-wage earners benefit from the minimum wage even when their households are supported by higher-wage earners. Under the wage-subsidy EITC, the higher-wage households are excluded from benefiting. For this reason, the wage-subsidy EITC is substantially less expensive, once we account for costs beyond those paid through the tax-transfer system.

The political attractiveness of the minimum wage arises from the fact that it is imposed as a regulation rather than treated as an income-transfer program. Because they are paid by consumers and shareholders, the costs of the program are dispersed and harder to link with the wage increase. Yet, as Table 5.3 shows, augmenting low wages through a wage-subsidy EITC has far lower overall cost than does augmenting low wages with a minimum-wage increase, precisely because of the targeting shown in Table 5.2.

6. Conclusions

This report explores a variety of options for a state EITC to inform policymakers about how program designs can influence the incomes and work incentives of poor families in California. Evaluating the effectiveness of an EITC program involves assessing three effects: (1) the program's total cost, (2) its targeting of benefits to needy families, and (3) the degree to which its benefits reward work. The California legislature most recently considered a 15 percent state supplement to the federal EITC. In addition to projecting the effectiveness of such an EITC, this report develops several alternatives devised to improve efficacy in achieving particular goals. Although this exercise illustrates the familiar lesson that no program is optimal for accomplishing all purposes, it also demonstrates that other designs are preferable to a simple supplement to the federal EITC.

A state program that merely supplements the federal EITC would come with considerable cost and would provide little in terms of income support or enhanced work incentives. A 15 percent state supplement would cost $732 million per year and provide average monthly benefits of only $25 to eligible families. Moreover, this EITC would enhance rewards to additional work for the lowest-wage families on CalWORKs by only 5 percent of their market wage, and it would actually discourage moderate- and high-wage families from leaving the CalWORKs rolls. For a comparable or lower expense, an EITC that bases benefits on both a family's earnings and measures of its hourly wages is preferable to any EITC in which benefits depend purely on total earnings. Whether delivered as a wage-based EITC—accounting for hours as well as earnings—or as a wage-subsidy EITC, these alternatives direct payments to families that are both low income and reliant upon low-wage employment; furthermore, these programs can create substantial rewards for additional work effort by working poor families both on and off welfare. The wage-subsidy EITC strategy most narrowly focuses on low-wage workers, rewarding work up to full-time employment with generous subsidies. However, the exact mechanism for this wage-subsidy EITC must be carefully crafted to avoid wage-subsidy disincentives for employers who may otherwise pay higher wages or for employees who may seek better employment or additional skills in the absence of such a program.

Part of the attractiveness of an add-on EITC is its administrative ease. In contrast, a wage-based EITC creates administrative challenges, with the most noteworthy being the assignment of hourly wages to families and the modification of employer tax reports to list approximations for hours worked as well as earnings. Such reporting used to be done in California when average wages were reported as part of the state's unemployment insurance program. In households with multiple earners, the individual wages must also be translated into a household average wage, but the properties of wage-subsidy EITCs do not appear to be very sensitive to the specific rule for assigning wages by family. In future deliberations over EITC policy, including those at the federal level, serious consideration should be given to designing programs that account for a family's hourly wages as well as its earnings in determining benefits.

Appendix

Detailed Findings on Distribution of Benefits under EITC Options

The tables at the end of this appendix elaborate on the findings reported in Chapter 5, providing detailed findings by family type for each option. In each table, the first column lists the demographic group included in each row's calculations. We examine seven families along seven key dimensions.

Family Structure

We start with a measure of all families with children, where children are defined as qualifying children under the current EITC rules. This qualifying child is usually a minor (i.e., a child below age 18) but also can be a college student. Within this heading, we select families with children under age 18 (that is, we exclude families that qualify only by having a college student). These families with minors are divided by whether they are married or single and then more specifically into families with single mothers and large families.

Income and Family Structure

The next two sets of rows examine families (with and without children) below the poverty threshold ("poor families") and below twice the poverty level (poor and near-poor families). Within these groups, we narrow the focus to families with children under age 18, again distinguishing by marital status of the household head. As an alternative income measure, we examine families in the bottom or bottom two quintiles of the income distribution. The lowest quintile consists of families whose incomes are in the lowest 20 percent of incomes for California families. The bottom two quintiles are for families in the bottom 40 percent of the income distribution. The poverty measure adjusts for family size but the quintile measure does not. In counting families below poverty or by quintile, we do *not* exclude families with no working members.

Hourly Wages

We next distinguish families with children based on their hourly wages. The first row indicates the characteristics of all families with children under age 18 who report any earnings. The following four rows divide working families into four exhaustive groups: (1) "Jobs paying below $7 per hour" includes families who receive 50 percent or more of their earnings from jobs paying $7 per hour or less; (2) "Jobs paying at most $9 per hour" designates families who receive 50 percent or more of their earnings from jobs paying $9 per hour or less and who cannot be included in the "below $7 per hour" group; (3) "Jobs paying at most $12 per hour" identifies families who receive 50 percent or more of their earnings from jobs paying $12 per hour or less and who cannot be included in either the "below $7 per hour" or the "below $9 per hour" groups; and (4) "Jobs paying over $12 per hour" signifies families who receive 50 percent or more of their earnings from jobs paying at least $12 per hour.

Annual Family Hours Worked

To capture the notion of "working poor" more accurately, the next set of rows divides families by the total number of hours worked. This total sums all hours worked in the year by all members of the family. Families with no working members are excluded. Conceptually, 2,000 hours is considered full-time work for one person, so the breakdown can be thought of as working less than one-quarter time (less than 500 hours), between quarter and half-time (between 500 and 1,000 hours), between half- and full-time (1,000 and 2,000 hours), and more than full-time (more than 2,000 hours).

Welfare Status

The last characteristic we consider is welfare status. We define welfare recipients as those receiving CalWORKs, SSI, or Food Stamps at any time during the calendar year. We then make the classification more specific by restricting to those who receive CalWORKs or SSI. Last, we report the effects of a program on those who receive Food Stamps but not CalWORKs or SSI.

Program Cost

The last line in each table lists our projected total costs of the program under consideration. We calculate this quantity by summing the benefits accrued to every family in the population, using sample weights to account for sample composition issues.

In addition to designating family characteristics, the columns of the appendix tables report various measures of the benefit distribution associated with each EITC option.

Composition of California Population

The column labeled "% All California Families" lists the percentage of all families in California that fall into the given demographic category. For example, the row labeled "Welfare Recipients with Children" shows the percentage of all California families that have children and receive some type of welfare.

Measures of Program Participation

The next two columns give two measures of program participation. "% Receiving Benefits" is the percentage of families who would be eligible to receive benefits. "% of Eligible Population" describes what share of all eligible families fall into that group. For example, in Table A.1, 37 percent of all California families with children under age 18 would receive benefits from the add-on EITC, and families with children under age 18 would account for 73 percent of all families who would be eligible for the add-on EITC.

Level and Share of Benefits

For families eligible to receive the EITC under each option, "Average Benefit" is the average credit amount received by families in that subgroup. Returning to our example from Table A.1, among families with children under age 18 who would benefit, the average amount that they are eligible for is $354.

Finally, "% of Benefits" describes what share of all dollar benefits received under the EITC option would go to families in this category. So, families with children under age 18 represent 73 percent of all eligible families, but they would receive 88 percent of all benefits under the add-on EITC (Table A.1).

Estimating Minimum-Wage Benefits and Costs

Our approach for determining the levels of increased earnings and distributional consequences attributable to a change in the minimum wage follows the methodology of MaCurdy and O'Brien-Strain (1998), O'Brien-Strain and MaCurdy (2000), and MaCurdy and McIntyre (2001). One can readily simulate the effects of increasing the minimum wage using the 1999 SIPP data by assuming that there are no employment effects, meaning that firms do not change their employment decisions with the introduction of a higher minimum wage. Under this no-job-loss assumption, calculating the benefits attributable to an increase in the state minimum wage from, say, $6.25 per hour to $6.75 per hour merely involves increasing the wage of every worker earning less than $6.75 per hour in the sample to $6.75. Given this change, it is straightforward to compute an individual's new earnings based upon his or her reported hours of work. The difference between these new earnings and an individual's real earnings is the benefit of the wage increase. Summing these benefits over all individuals within a family gives the family's total minimum-wage increase benefit level. There is one further necessary calculation because minimum-wage benefits are pretax, in contrast to the after-tax EITC benefits. Accordingly, the calculations deduct taxes from the extra earnings generated by the minimum-wage increase and assign this as an after-tax benefit to the family. Even if the family is earning too little to pay income taxes, it still pays payroll taxes on any incremental minimum-wage earnings. Consequently, this discussion reports minimum-wage benefits after taxes (which makes sense as these are the only benefits that a family really cares about). Finally, the analysis examines how these extra dollars are allocated across families as described above in the case of EITC benefits.

In these computations, the analysis presumes that all workers earn an hourly wage equal to at least $6.25 per hour in 2001 dollars, discounted into 1999 dollars; the resulting level closely approximates the actual value of California's minimum wage in 1999 ($5.75 per hour in 1999 dollars).[1] We estimated the change in wages from the move both to $6.75 and to $7.50. The benefit calculations for the minimum wage are after-tax benefits, accounting for payroll taxes and state and federal income taxes. The total cost of the program includes both the after-tax benefits and the additional tax revenues. As the EITC benefits are not taxed, the distinction is irrelevant to the EITC programs.

---

[1]Thus, when considering the change from $6.25 to $6.75, persons in 1999 earning $6.25 per hour or less in 2001 dollars had their hourly wages boosted by $0.50. If a worker earns between $6.25 and $6.75 per hour in 2001 dollars, then this person receives the difference between his or her hourly wage and $6.75. When entertaining a change in the minimum wage from $6.25 to $7.50, persons in 1999 earning $6.25 per hour or less in 2001 dollars had their hourly wages raised by $1.25. This is like assuming that everyone was at least at the old minimum wage before moving up. The analysis does the same thing when calculating benefits under alternative EITC schemes so the comparison among the options remains valid.

Table A.1

Distribution of Benefits Across Families from a 15 Percent California Add-On to the Federal EITC (Projections for 2001)

Family Characteristics	% of All California Families	Benefits from an Earnings-Based EITC			
		% Receiving Benefits	% of Eligible Population	Average Benefit ($)	% Share of Total Benefits
Families with qualifying children	43	38	83	305	98
With children under age 18	39	37	73	312	88
Married	27	28	39	335	50
Single	12	55	35	287	38
Female-headed	9	58	26	289	29
3 or more children	10	47	25	366	35
Income below poverty level	14	48	34	322	42
With children under age 18	7	75	25	394	38
Married	3	93	13	478	24
Single	4	61	12	302	14
Income below twice poverty level	34	45	77	290	86
With children under age 18	15	78	59	341	78
Married	8	80	33	355	45
Single	7	74	27	323	33
Income in lowest 20% of families	20	32	32	248	31
With children under age 18	5	69	18	356	25
Married	1	89	6	476	11
Single	4	62	12	297	14
Income in lowest 40% of families	40	36	72	282	79
With children under age 18	13	83	53	341	70
Married	5	94	26	379	38
Single	7	74	27	305	32

Table A.1 (continued)

Family Characteristics	% of All California Families	Benefits from an Earnings-Based EITC			
		% Receiving Benefits	% of Eligible Population	Average Benefit ($)	% Share of Total Benefits
Families with children and earnings	37	38	73	313	88
50% family earnings from					
Jobs paying below $7 per hour	5	89	23	357	31
Jobs paying at most $9 per hour	4	85	19	364	26
Jobs paying at most $12 per hour	5	64	17	279	19
Jobs paying over $12 per hour	23	12	14	217	12
Work effort of families with children					
Family's annual hours					
Below 500	3	26	4	101	2
500–1,000	2	75	6	304	7
1,000–2,000	4	71	15	408	24
Above 2,000	30	31	48	302	55
Welfare recipients with children	7	62	22	354	30
CalWORKs or SSI	6	59	17	350	23
Food Stamps only	1	78	4	371	6
Projected annual costs					$732 million

Table A.2

Distribution of Benefits Across Families from a Low-Earnings EITC (Projections for 2001)

Family Characteristics	% of All California Families	% Receiving Benefits	Benefits from a Wage-Subsidy EITC		
			% of Eligible Population	Average Benefit ($)	% Share of Total Benefits
Families with qualifying children	43	22	79	249	97
With children under age 18	39	21	68	258	87
Married	27	15	33	288	46
Single	12	35	35	231	40
Female-headed	9	39	28	229	32
3 or more children	10	31	26	307	40
Income below poverty level	14	46	52	240	61
With children under age 18	7	71	38	289	55
Married	3	86	19	338	32
Single	4	60	19	240	23
Income below twice poverty level	34	31	84	219	91
With children under age 18	15	50	61	266	80
Married	8	45	29	296	42
Single	7	56	32	239	38
Income in lowest 20% of families	20	30	48	202	48
With children under age 18	5	68	29	274	39
Married	1	89	10	359	17
Single	4	61	19	231	22
Income in lowest 40% of families	40	25	79	215	84
With children under age 18	13	54	55	268	73
Married	5	57	25	293	37
Single	7	51	30	246	36

Table A.2 (continued)

Family Characteristics	% of All California Families	Benefits from a Wage-Subsidy EITC			
		% Receiving Benefits	% of Eligible Population	Average Benefit ($)	% Share of Total Benefits
Families with children and earnings	37	22	67	260	86
50% family earnings from					
Jobs paying below $7 per hour	5	74	30	277	41
Jobs paying at most $9 per hour	4	55	19	263	25
Jobs paying at most $12 per hour	5	23	10	233	12
Jobs paying over $12 per hour	23	4	8	218	8
Work effort of families with children					
Family's annual hours					
Below 500	3	26	7	101	3
500–1,000	2	73	9	264	12
1,000–2,000	4	55	19	334	31
Above 2,000	30	13	32	247	39
Welfare recipients with children	7	52	29	271	39
CalWORKs or SSI	6	52	24	271	32
Food Stamps only	1	55	5	272	7
Projected annual costs	$358 million				

Table A.3

Distribution of Benefits Across Families from a High-Earnings EITC (Projections for 2001)

Family Characteristics	% of All California Families	% Receiving Benefits	After-Tax Benefits from a Minimum Wage		
			% of Eligible Population	Average Benefit ($)	% Share of Total Benefits
Families with qualifying children	43	26	74	256	97
With children under age 18	39	26	67	266	90
Married	27	22	40	275	57
Single	12	32	26	252	34
Female-headed	9	34	20	244	25
3 or more children	10	34	23	287	34
Income below poverty level	14	24	22	228	26
With children under age 18	7	41	18	268	24
Married	3	70	13	280	18
Single	4	20	5	238	6
Income below twice poverty level	34	35	78	215	85
With children under age 18	15	56	55	281	79
Married	8	66	35	288	51
Single	7	44	21	268	28
Income in lowest 20% of families	20	23	30	101	15
With children under age 18	5	32	11	196	11
Married	1	54	5	204	5
Single	4	24	6	189	6
Income in lowest 40% of families	40	28	72	201	74
With children under age 18	13	57	48	278	67
Married	5	78	28	295	42
Single	7	41	19	253	25

Table A.3 (continued)

Family Characteristics	% of All California Families	After-Tax Benefits from a Minimum Wage			
		% Receiving Benefits	% of Eligible Population	Average Benefit ($)	% Share of Total Benefits
Families with children and earnings	37	27	67	266	90
50% family earnings from					
Jobs paying below $7 per hour	5	55	18	237	22
Jobs paying at most $9 per hour	4	66	19	288	27
Jobs paying at most $12 per hour	5	49	17	300	26
Jobs paying over $12 per hour	23	8	13	229	15
Work effort of families with children					
Family's annual hours					
Below 500	3	0	0	.	0
500–1,000	2	21	2	200	2
1,000–2,000	4	53	15	226	17
Above 2,000	30	25	50	281	71
Welfare recipients with children	7	36	17	250	21
CalWORKs or SSI	6	32	12	242	15
Food Stamps only	1	62	5	271	6
Projected annual costs				$427 million	

Table A.4

Distribution of Benefits Across Families from a Wage-Based EITC (Projections for 2001)

Family Characteristics	% of All California Families	Benefits from a Wage-Based EITC			
		% Receiving Benefits	% of Eligible Population	Average Benefit ($)	% Share of Total Benefits
Families with qualifying children	43	35	100	256	100
With children under age 18	39	34	88	268	92
Married	27	27	47	296	54
Single	12	52	41	236	38
Female-headed	9	54	31	232	28
3 or more children	10	44	29	321	37
Income below poverty level	14	40	36	297	41
With children under age 18	7	72	31	321	39
Married	3	89	16	402	25
Single	4	60	15	235	14
Income below twice poverty level	34	37	81	276	87
With children under age 18	15	74	72	289	82
Married	8	77	40	312	48
Single	7	72	33	260	33
Income in lowest 20% of families	20	23	29	246	28
With children under age 18	5	68	23	268	24
Married	1	86	7	371	11
Single	4	61	15	218	13
Income in lowest 40% of families	40	29	74	270	78
With children under age 18	13	80	65	285	72
Married	5	90	32	328	41
Single	7	71	33	244	32

Table A.4 (continued)

Family Characteristics	% of All California Families	Benefits from a Wage-Based EITC			
		% Receiving Benefits	% of Eligible Population	Average Benefit ($)	% Share of Total Benefits
Families with children and earnings	37	36	87	269	92
50% family earnings from					
Jobs paying below $7 per hour	5	88	29	326	37
Jobs paying at most $9 per hour	4	85	24	311	29
Jobs paying at most $12 per hour	5	64	22	233	20
Jobs paying over $12 per hour	23	9	13	129	7
Work effort of families with children					
Family's annual hours					
Below 500	3	23	5	48	1
500–1,000	2	69	7	157	4
1,000–2,000	4	66	18	302	21
Above 2,000	30	29	57	290	65
Welfare recipients with children	7	58	26	300	30
CalWORKs or SSI	6	54	20	297	23
Food Stamps only	1	77	6	311	7
Projected annual costs		$570 million			

75

Table A.5

Distribution of Benefits Across Families from a $7.50 Wage-Subsidy EITC with Phaseout (Projections for 2001)

Family Characteristics	% of All California Families	% Receiving Benefits	Benefits from a Wage-Based EITC		
			% of Eligible Population	Average Benefit ($)	% Share of Total Benefits
Families with qualifying children	43	14	100	1,241	100
With children under age 18	39	13	85	1,248	85
Married	27	10	44	1,392	50
Single	12	20	40	1,091	36
Female-headed	9	23	34	1,052	29
3 or more children	10	19	33	1,242	33
Income below poverty level	14	25	59	1,206	57
With children under age 18	7	46	52	1,228	51
Married	3	53	25	1,660	33
Single	4	42	27	842	19
Income below twice poverty level	34	16	93	1,240	93
With children under age 18	15	32	80	1,249	81
Married	8	30	40	1,417	46
Single	7	34	40	1,081	35
Income in lowest 20% of families	20	16	52	1,177	50
With children under age 18	5	49	43	1,154	40
Married	1	62	14	1,604	18
Single	4	45	29	939	22
Income in lowest 40% of families	40	13	85	1,265	87
With children under age 18	13	34	73	1,279	75
Married	5	37	34	1,519	41
Single	7	32	39	1,073	34

Table A.5 (continued)

Family Characteristics	% of All California Families	Benefits from a Wage-Based EITC			
		% Receiving Benefits	% of Eligible Population	Average Benefit ($)	% Share of Total Benefits
	37	13	84	1,257	85
Families with children and earnings					
50% family earnings from					
Jobs paying below $7 per hour	5	77	66	1,296	69
Jobs paying at most $9 per hour	4	23	16	1,028	14
Jobs paying at most $12 per hour	5	2	2	1,796	2
Jobs paying over $12 per hour	23	0	0	2,175	1
Work effort of families with children					
Family's annual hours					
Below 500	3	15	8	204	1
500–1,000	2	41	11	657	6
1,000–2,000	4	36	25	1,385	28
Above 2,000	30	8	40	1,539	49
Welfare recipients with children	7	33	38	1,178	36
CalWORKs or SSI	6	34	33	1,129	30
Food Stamps only	1	31	6	1,458	7
Projected annual costs		$1,063 million			

Table A.6

Distribution of Benefits Across Families from a $7.50 Wage-Subsidy EITC Without Phaseout (Projections for 2001)

Family Characteristics	% of All California Families	% Receiving Benefits	Benefits from a Wage-Based EITC — % of Eligible Population	Average Benefit ($)	% Share of Total Benefits
Families with qualifying children	43	16	100	1,399	100
With children under age 18	39	15	87	1,406	87
Married	27	12	48	1,625	56
Single	12	22	38	1,131	31
Female-headed	9	24	31	1,085	24
3 or more children	10	22	32	1,454	33
Income below poverty level	14	26	51	1,263	46
With children under age 18	7	48	45	1,288	42
Married	3	53	21	1,775	26
Single	4	44	24	870	15
Income below twice poverty level	34	19	89	1,383	88
With children under age 18	15	37	79	1,397	79
Married	8	36	41	1,664	49
Single	7	37	37	1,103	29
Income in lowest 20% of families	20	16	45	1,222	39
With children under age 18	5	50	37	1,204	32
Married	1	62	12	1,666	14
Single	4	45	25	986	18
Income in lowest 40% of families	40	14	80	1,356	77
With children under age 18	13	38	69	1,368	67
Married	5	42	33	1,685	39
Single	7	35	36	1,083	28

Table A.6 (continued)

Family Characteristics	% of All California Families	Benefits from a Wage-Based EITC			
		% Receiving Benefits	% of Eligible Population	Average Benefit ($)	% Share of Total Benefits
Families with children and earnings	37	16	86	1,414	87
50% family earnings from					
Jobs paying below $7 per hour	5	87	63	1,558	70
Jobs paying at most $9 per hour	4	33	21	990	15
Jobs paying at most $12 per hour	5	3	2	1,302	2
Jobs paying over $12 per hour	23	0	0	1,310	0
Work effort of families with children					
Family's annual hours					
Below 500	3	16	7	399	2
500–1,000	2	43	10	626	4
1,000–2,000	4	36	21	1,414	22
Above 2,000	30	11	47	1,730	58
Welfare recipients with children	7	35	35	1,279	32
CalWORKs or SSI	6	36	29	1,239	26
Food Stamps only	1	33	5	1,506	6
Projected annual costs		$1,408 million			

79

Table A.7
Distribution of Benefits Across Families from a $7.50 Minimum Wage (Projections for 2001)

Family Characteristics	% of All California Families	Benefits from a Wage-Based EITC			
		% Receiving Benefits	% of Eligible Population	Average Benefit ($)	% Share of Total Benefits
Families with qualifying children	43	63	59	759	67
With children under age 18	39	62	53	747	59
Married	27	63	37	735	41
Single	12	59	16	776	18
Female-headed	9	57	11	773	13
3 or more children	10	68	15	865	19
Income below poverty level	14	45	13	1,033	21
With children under age 18	7	64	9	1,055	14
Married	3	77	5	1,245	9
Single	4	54	5	863	6
Income below twice poverty level	34	50	36	1,031	56
With children under age 18	15	69	22	1,092	36
Married	8	75	13	1,205	23
Single	7	61	9	934	13
Income in lowest 20% of families	20	41	18	982	26
With children under age 18	5	63	7	1,006	11
Married	1	84	2	1,319	5
Single	4	55	5	843	6
Income in lowest 40% of families	40	45	38	865	49
With children under age 18	13	64	18	1,001	26
Married	5	73	9	1,151	15
Single	7	58	9	855	11

Table A.7 (continued)

Family Characteristics	% of All California Families	Benefits from a Wage-Based EITC			
		% Receiving Benefits	% of Eligible Population	Average Benefit ($)	% Share of Total Benefits
Families with children and earnings	37	65	53	749	59
50% family earnings from					
Jobs paying below $7 per hour	5	100	11	1,713	28
Jobs paying at most $9 per hour	4	84	8	763	9
Jobs paying at most $12 per hour	5	66	8	689	8
Jobs paying over $12 per hour	23	54	26	362	14
Work effort of families with children					
Family's annual hours					
Below 500	3	29	2	300	1
500–1,000	2	75	3	594	2
1,000–2,000	4	70	6	814	8
Above 2,000	30	63	42	768	48
Welfare recipients with children	7	64	10	1,061	15
CalWORKs or SSI	6	63	8	1,054	12
Food Stamps only	1	71	2	1,093	3
Projected annual costs	$4,469 million in after-tax earnings and $1,040 million in taxes				

Table A.8

Distribution of Benefits Across Families from a $7.50 Wage-Subsidy EITC with Phaseout Where Those Without Qualifying Children Receive Benefits (Projections for 2001)

Family Characteristics	% of All California Families	% Receiving Benefits	Benefits from a Wage-Based EITC		
			% of Eligible Population	Average Benefit ($)	% Share of Total Benefits
Families with qualifying children	43	29	69	1,246	69
With children under age 18	39	28	59	1,247	59
Married	27	25	36	1,300	38
Single	12	34	23	1,161	21
Female-headed	9	35	17	1,040	14
3 or more children	10	35	20	1,278	20
Income below poverty level	14	37	28	1,125	25
With children under age 18	7	52	19	1,279	19
Married	3	59	9	1,730	12
Single	4	46	10	868	7
Income below twice poverty level	34	34	62	1,360	67
With children under age 18	15	45	37	1,432	42
Married	8	46	20	1,651	26
Single	7	44	17	1,173	16
Income in lowest 20% of families	20	33	35	1,221	34
With children under age 18	5	52	15	1,197	14
Married	1	66	5	1,635	6
Single	4	47	10	984	8
Income in lowest 40% of families	40	27	57	1,286	59
With children under age 18	13	44	30	1,334	32
Married	5	48	14	1,607	18
Single	7	40	16	1,090	14

Table A.8 (continued)

Family Characteristics	% of All California Families	Benefits from a Wage-Based EITC			
		% Receiving Benefits	% of Eligible Population	Average Benefit ($)	% Share of Total Benefits
Families with children and earnings	37	29	59	1,251	59
50% family earnings from					
Jobs paying below $7 per hour	5	96	26	1,718	36
Jobs paying at most $9 per hour	4	48	11	1,013	9
Jobs paying at most $12 per hour	5	18	5	993	4
Jobs paying over $12 per hour	23	13	16	748	10
Work effort of families with children					
Family's annual hours					
Below 500	3	26	4	339	1
500–1,000	2	52	4	580	2
1,000–2,000	4	41	9	1,348	10
Above 2,000	30	25	40	1,399	45
Welfare recipients with children	7	45	17	1,252	17
CalWORKs or SSI	6	45	14	1,245	14
Food Stamps only	1	47	3	1,289	3
Projected annual costs		$3,314 million			

Bibliography

Blank, Rebecca, David Card, and Philip K. Robins, "Financial Incentives for Increasing Work and Income among Low-Income Families," in Rebecca Blank and David Card, eds., *Finding Work: Jobs and Welfare Reform,* Russell Sage, New York, 2000.

Burkhauser, Richard V., and T. Aldrich Finegan, "The Minimum Wage and the Poor: The End of a Relationship," *Journal of Policy Analysis and Management,* Vol. 8, No. 1, 1989, pp. 53–71.

Burkhauser, Richard V., Kenneth A. Couch, and Andrew J. Glenn, "Public Policies for the Working Poor: The Earned Income Tax Credit versus Minimum Wage Legislation," *Research in Labor Economics,* Vol. 15, 1996, pp. 65–109.

Burkhauser, Richard V., Kenneth A. Couch, and David C. Wittenburg, "Who Gets What from Minimum Wage Hikes: A Re-Estimation of Card and Krueger's Distributional Analysis in Myth and Measurement: The New Economics of the Minimum Wage," *Industrial and Labor Relations Review,* Vol. 49, No. 3, 1996, pp. 547–552.

Eissa, Nada, and Hilary Williamson Hoynes, "The Earned Income Tax Credit and the Labor Supply of Married Couples," NBER Working Paper No. 6856, Cambridge, Massachusetts, 1998.

Hotz, V. Joseph, Charles Mullin, and John Karl Scholz, "The EITC and Low-Wage Labor Markets in California," Joint Center for Poverty Research Conference Paper, Washington, D.C., December 7–8, 2000.

Johnson, Nicholas, *A Hand-Up: How State Earned Income Tax Credits Help Working Poor Families Escape Poverty,* Center on Budget and Policy Priorities, Washington, D.C., 1999, available at www.cbpp.org.

Johnson, Nicholas, *How Much Would a State Earned Income Tax Credit Cost?* Center on Budget and Policy Priorities, Washington, D.C., April 28, 2003, available at www.cbpp.org.

Johnson, William R., and Edgar K. Browning, "The Distributional and Efficiency Effects of Increasing the Minimum Wage: A Simulation," *American Economic Review,* Vol. 73, 1983, pp. 204–211.

Keeley, Michael C., Philip K. Robins, Robert G. Spiegelman, and Richard W. West, "The Labor Supply Effects and Costs of Alternative Negative Income Tax Programs," *Journal of Human Resources*, Vol. 13, No. 1, 1978, pp. 3–36.

MaCurdy, Thomas, and Margaret O'Brien-Strain, "Who Benefits and Who Pays for Minimum Wages in California? A Perspective on Proposition 210," *Essays in Public Policy*, Hoover Press, 1998.

MaCurdy, Thomas, and Frank McIntyre, "Winners and Losers of Federal and State Minimum Wages," Stanford Institute for Economic Policy Research, Stanford, California, 2001.

Madden, Nan, "Minnesota: Expansion of State Tax Credit Makes Work Pay for Welfare Families," *Poverty Research News,* Vol. 3, No. 1, Joint Center for Poverty Research, Chicago, Illinois, 1999.

Meyer, Bruce, and Dan Rosenbaum, "Making Single Mothers Work: Recent Tax and Welfare Policy and Its Effects," Mimeo, Northwestern University, Evanston, Illinois, 1999.

Neumark, David, and William Wascher, "The Effects of the Minimum Wage, Welfare, and the EITC on Family Incomes," Joint Center for Poverty Research Conference Paper, 1999.

O'Brien-Strain, Margaret, and Thomas MaCurdy, *Increasing the Minimum Wage: California's Winners and Losers,* Public Policy Institute of California, San Francisco, California, 2000.

Robins, Philip K., and Charles Michalopoulos, "The Effects of Financial Incentives for Welfare Recipients: Evidence from Microsimulation," Joint Center for Poverty Research Conference Paper, Washington, D.C., December 7–8, 2000.

About the Author

THOMAS E. MACURDY

Thomas MaCurdy is an adjunct fellow at PPIC, a professor of economics at Stanford University, and a senior fellow at the Hoover Institution. His principal research explores topics in the areas of income transfer programs, human resources, and labor markets. His recent studies investigate the consequences of governmental policies underlying welfare programs, unemployment compensation, Social Security, Medicare, Medicaid, and various forms of public assistance for low-income populations. He holds an A.B. from the University of Washington and a Ph.D. in economics from the University of Chicago.

Related PPIC Publications

Does California's Welfare Policy Explain the Slower Decline of Its Caseload?
Thomas E. MaCurdy, David C. Mancuso, and Margaret O'Brien-Strain

What Happens to Families When They Leave Welfare?
Thomas MaCurdy, Grecia Marrufo, and Margaret O'Brien-Strain

How Living Wage Laws Affect Low-Income Workers and Low-Income Families
David Neumark

Increasing the Minimum Wage: California's Winners and Losers
Margaret O'Brien-Strain and Thomas MaCurdy

California's Rising Income Inequality: Causes and Concerns
Deborah Reed

"Recent Trends in Income and Poverty"
California Counts: Population Trends and Profiles
Volume 5, Number 3, February 2004
Deborah Reed

PPIC publications may be ordered by phone or from our website
(800) 232-5343 [mainland U.S.]
(415) 291-4400 [Canada, Hawaii, overseas]
www.ppic.org